"Insightful, entertaining and useful! Maister's work bridges the gap between theory and practice; grounded in conceptual bedrock, it offers practical 'Monday morning' advice for anyone involved in managing a professional service firm."

—Thomas J. Tierney, Worldwide Managing Director,
Bain & Company

"David Maister is the guru of professional services. A routine reading of Maister's lessons is good religion for all practice managers."

—John Harvey, Chairman, PriceWaterhouseCoopers, Australia

"*True Professionalism* is pure gold. You'll be able to mine this rich vein for your entire career and always discover another nugget."

—James M. Kouzes, coauthor of
The Leadership Challenge and *Credibility*

"Maister is not for the fainthearted. If you are not prepared to ask the tough questions about your business, don't open this book!"

—Adrian Martin, Managing Partner, BDO Stoy Hayward UK

"Maister's ideas are applicable in a wide range of professional businesses and are equally valid for small firms or large. This book speaks to the professional in all of us."

—Tom Watson, Vice Chairman, Omnicom Group, Inc.

"Provocative, controversial and stimulating, Maister challenges traditional thinking and provides new insights on a wide range of important issues."

—Martin Sorrell, Chairman, WPP Group plc

"David Maister has a keen awareness of what creates success in professional service firms and a clear way of communicating ideas that truly make a difference."

—A. W. (Pete) Smith, Jr., President & CEO, Watson Wyatt Worldwide

"Maister in print, like Maister in person, is animated, entertaining and insightful. He always leaves the reader with food for further thought."

—John M. Westcott, Jr., Assistant Managing Partner,
Hale & Dorr, Boston

"David Maister is a walking oxymoron, a practical visionary whose thoughtful analysis of the professional service firm is must-reading for anyone trying to lead, manage or survive in one. If you need help getting your prima donnas to sing like a chorus, read this book—better yet, ask them to."

—Robert M. Heller, Kramer, Levin, Naftalis & Frankel

"David Maister's knowledge of professional services is second to none."

—Fergus Ryan, Managing Partner,
Arthur Andersen, Australia

"David Maister combines knowledge, insights, and intellectual honesty with good humor. You may not always agree with him, but he will always make you think."

—Lawrence Gerber, McDermott, Will & Emery

"David Maister has the unique ability to tell you how to apply management principles in a practical way. It seems that every article contained a bit of wisdom that proved important in managing our law firm."

—John W. Larson, Brobeck, Phleger & Harrison LLP

"This high-density book contains what a manager seldom takes time to think about. It is a monument of wisdom, as well as a sophisticated global vision of the professional firms."

—Bernard Courtaud, Groupe Courtaud, France

"Maister teaches us how to overcome the apparent contradiction between management consulting as a profession and/or as a business. His book is of high practical value to top management of large consulting firms, as well as to individual practitioners."

—Roland Berger, Chairman of the Board,
Roland Berger & Partners GmbH, Germany

"David Maister's writings are so clear, so good and so relevant that I'm tempted to hope that our competitors will not read them. If they do, there will be an unavoidable urge to act and to strive for better professional lives for themselves and for their firms."

—Louis H. van Lennep, DeBrauw Blackstone Westbroek, Netherlands

TRUE
PROFESSIONALISM

The Courage to Care About
Your People, Your Clients, and Your Career

DAVID H. MAISTER

A Touchstone Book
Published by Simon & Schuster
New York   London   Toronto   Sydney

TOUCHSTONE
Rockefeller Center
1230 Avenue of the Americas
New York, NY 10020

First Touchstone Edition 2000
TOUCHSTONE and colophon are registered trademarks
of Simon & Schuster, Inc.

Manufactured in the United States of America

20   19   18   17   16   15   14   13   12

The Library of Congress has cataloged the Free Press edition as follows:

Maister, David H.
    True professionalism: the courage to care about your people,
your clients, and your career/ David H. Maister.
        p.   cm.
    Includes index.
    1. Professions.   2. Professional employees.   3. Self-employed.
    4. Success in business.   I. Title.
    HD8038.A1M35   1997
    650.1—dc21   96–51994
                                                        CIP

ISBN   0-684-83466-9 (alk. paper)
        0-684-84004-9 (Pbk.)

Copyright on all of the work in this book is held by the author. Nevertheless, grateful acknowledgment is made to the journals that, between 1993 and 1996, published earlier versions of the following chapters herein: "Real Professionalism" (in *Legal Business,* October 1995); "Are You Having Fun Yet?" (in *The American Lawyer,* June 1994);

Continued on page 210

As it is for all that I do,
this is for Kathy

CONTENTS

PART THREE: (MOSTLY) ABOUT YOUR CLIENTS

ACKNOWLEDGMENTS

First and foremost, to my consulting clients around the world: Thank you! You gave me the chance to explore ideas with you, permission to challenge sometimes sacred beliefs, and (even when you did not agree) the encouragement to keep thinking and working alongside you! I appreciate the opportunities you provided.

I must also acknowledge the wise counsel of Kathy Maister, my wife. As we have traveled the world together, we have had many conversations in remote hotels, airports, and airplanes about my client experiences, my ideas, and my various successes and failures in attempting to communicate those ideas. These conversations have been invaluable in helping me make sense of my professional life. Experience is a great teacher, if you've got a good guide to help you extract the right lessons from it. Kathy is a terrific guide—one who knows how to ask the right question at the right time and, perhaps most importantly, in the right way.

Next, I need to stress Julie O'Leary's significant contribution. Apart from being an outstanding business manager, Julie serves as my editor. She gives an in-depth reading to everything that I write, to ensure that the content makes sense, that it flows reasonably, and that I adhere (at least approximately) to the accepted rules of grammar, spelling, and punctuation. It is not until she has given her recommendations on an article (recommendations that I almost always accept) that I send it out into the world. Her fingerprints are all over this book, and it is all the better for her input.

Patrick McKenna and Gerry Riskin, of The Edge Group, with whom I have prepared a series of self-directed training programs (including videotapes), provided useful reactions and suggestions to many of the concepts discussed in this book.

I am very grateful to the journals that provided an outlet for the articles that form the chapters of this book. Two journals in particular, *The American Lawyer* and *Legal Business,* first provided me the impetus to get many of the pieces that appear here written and published, and thus the opportunity to disseminate them to other professions. I also appreciate their willingness to let me write about professional service firms and not restrict myself to law firms.

David H. Maister
Maister Associates, Inc.
P.O. Box 946
Boston, MA 02117
Tel: 617-262-5968
Fax: 617-262-7907
Website: http://www.davidmaister.com
E-mail: David_Maister@msn.com

INTRODUCTION:
THE POWER OF PRINCIPLES

> The Saints did not pray to the Good Lord for instruc-
> tion on what to do. The Bible was already clear on what
> was expected of them. Nevertheless, the Saints got
> down on their knees every day of their lives—to pray
> that, in spite of daily temptations, they could find the
> courage and strength to *do* the right thing.
>
> —*Old Mexican Proverb*

There are relatively few new ideas in business, if any at all. How often can one repeat the basic advice of "Listen to your clients, provide outstanding service, train your people, look for and eliminate inefficiencies, and act like team players?" The problem, clearly, is not in figuring out what to do. Rather, the problem is to find the strength and courage to do what we know to be right.

Professional firms expend immense efforts trying to get their people to do the "right" things through systems, structures, and monetary incentives. Not only have all of these frequently failed to create excellence, but they also leave a bad taste in the mouth. "Do it and we'll pay you" smacks more of prostitution than of professionalism. In discussing recommended courses of action with my consulting clients, I repeatedly find myself saying "This is not only good business, but it's the professional, ethical thing to do!" When something is presented as

1

When something is presented as a management tactic, it is easy to argue with and dismiss. It is harder to argue with a matter of *principle*.

a management tactic, it is easy to argue with and dismiss. It is harder to argue with a matter of *principle*.

Principles (or values) are the most effective management tools a firm can use. Successful firms are differentiated not by their different goals, clever strategies, or special managerial tactics—these are all remarkably similar worldwide. Successful firms *are* clearly differentiated by a strict adherence to values, i.e., to professionalism.

Do You Maximize or Minimize the Bill?

An example will illustrate the point. Any firm that emphasizes and rewards its professionals for large amounts of personal billable hours (or "utilization") creates an incentive for people to find ways to maximize the bill on every engagement (perhaps even subconsciously) in order to get credit for as many billable hours as possible. Not surprisingly, clients are increasingly suspicious that this system encourages inefficiency, since the more time it takes the professional to do the work, the more the professional gets paid. (In the practice of law, for example, some corporate clients now hire firms of "legal bill auditors" to examine their outside lawyers' bills for waste, inefficiency and, in extremely rare cases, fraud.)

Clearly, the ethical and professional thing to do, as the client's agent, is to work hard in order to achieve the client's goals at the *minimum* possible cost to the client on each transaction. It is one thing to charge high fees for productive work. It is an entirely different matter to be inefficient and waste client resources on unnecessary or unproductive activities.

A true professional feels no pressure to run up a client's bill, knowing that any reduction in revenues caused by being efficient will be more than recompensed by the reputation earned for being honest and trustworthy. A provider that is not efficient in spending the client's money soon loses the client's trust and confidence.

Is this an ethical point or a "good business" point? Of course, it is both. Either argument leads to the same conclusion: A good reputation is more valuable than extra income earned through inefficiency. One would like to believe that this is obvious. However, it often happens that when I make this point, many professionals are skeptical. They frequently ask: "How long does it take for the market to recognize your trustworthiness and efficiency and then reward you with new business?" The answer is "very quickly." Clients are intelligent people and, because they usually employ more than one provider, they can easily recognize differences in quality, cost, service, and attitude. They can, and do, move their business around quickly and reward efficiency promptly.

Evoking the moral argument is not necessary, although it's still the real one. One should be efficient not only because it's good business, but because it's the right thing to do. Doing the right thing *is* good business! Yet one still hears the argument in professional firms that "I know what I'm doing could be done by a less costly person, but if I delegate it to someone who charges less than I do, our revenues will go down." Do people making this argument need a lesson in business or a lesson in professional ethics?

> **Evoking the moral argument is not necessary, although it's still the real one. One should be efficient not only because it's good business, but because it's the right thing to do.**

Supervising Client Projects

Another example is found when supervising client engagements. In my book *Managing the Professional Service Firm* (The Free Press, 1993), I suggested asking junior professionals about their experience on work assignments and whether or not it was usually true that:

1. When tasks and projects were assigned, they understood thoroughly what was expected of them.
2. They understood how their tasks fit into the overall objectives for the engagement.
3. They were kept informed about the things they needed to know in order to do their jobs properly.

4. They received good coaching to help improve performance.
5. They received *prompt* feedback on their work, good or bad.
6. They felt that they were a member of a well-functioning team.

Every time I discuss this idea with professionals, I ask them what benefits might come from achieving excellence in these areas (i.e., doing all the above thoroughly, every single time). They always provide the following list:

1. Motivated staff
2. Better quality work-product
3. Better trained, skilled staff
4. Less wasted time
5. Lower "write-offs" of unproductive work that can't be billed
6. More timely delivery of work
7. Greater ability to delegate since staff will be better trained
8. Free up partner time to focus on high-value-added activities
9. Clients would notice better service, more teamwork, more motivation

Quality, efficiency, higher profits, and client service. Not a bad list of benefits! The business case for doing well in this area is clear. A little bit of extra time invested in supervising would reap large financial (and nonfinancial) benefits. However, many professionals remain skeptical and argue that they are too busy to do all this, and they point out that "clients won't pay for supervision time."

Apart from the fact that this is faulty business reasoning (the return on investment for good supervision is huge), there is a profound *moral* issue here. Clients entrust professionals with their affairs. In effect, they say, "Here's my baby, please look after my baby!" As the professional service provider, you cannot say, "Well, *I* did the right thing. It was the junior staff who dropped the baby on its head."

Diligence in supervising a client's transaction is an ethical issue, a matter of responsibility for due care.

When you accept an assignment from a client, good supervision is not optional. Rather, diligence in supervising a client's transaction is an ethical issue, a matter of responsibility for due care. It's about professional responsibility and true professionalism. The fact that it's the high profit thing to do is wonderful, but you should do it because its the right thing to do. Nevertheless, in most professional firms, excellence in project supervision remains the exception rather than the rule.

Caring for Clients

A final example might help. In Chapter 17, I point out that whenever a professional is trying to sell something, there is only one question on the client's mind: "Why are you trying to sell me something?" There are two possible conclusions the client could come to: First, he or she might believe that the professional is trying to sell something just to get more revenues. Or, second, the client might believe that the professional is trying to sell something because he or she is interested in the client, truly cares, and is sincerely trying to help.

Under what conditions is the sale made? Even if you leave the moral argument aside, it should be clear that new business will be won only to the extent that the client believes that the professional is interested, cares, and is trying to help. Again, the noble path wins. One could argue that the professional's task is to make the client *think* that the professional cares, i.e., professionals must learn how to fake sincerity. (Indeed,

> New business will be won only to the extent that the client believes that the professional is interested, cares, and is trying to help.

many sales training courses in professional firms are filled with such tips and tactics.) However, faking sincerity is a prostitute's tactic, not a professional's. It may work occasionally, but not as often as real sincerity.

Is this moral counsel or business advice? Either way, the conclusion is the same. You will get hired, rehired, obtain referrals, and have lessened fee sensitivity to the extent that you care passionately, both about your work and your clients. The only remaining question for the professional is whether or not he or she has the courage to do so.

What Is Professionalism?

This book, although it covers many topics, is mainly about professionalism. I begin with a few reflections on "having fun" and "continual self-improvement" because I believe that true professionalism means the pursuit of excellence, not just competence. Many professionals confess that they are "cruising" below their full potential, and few feel passionate about the majority of their work. Many professionals, I have learned, are *not* having fun. Low morale and enthusiasm are common.

In significant part, this situation has resulted directly from the financial measures firms have used, especially the emphasis on "production," which measures only the volume of work, and not its caliber. The prevailing ethos in many firms is "It's about the money, stupid!" Strict financial controls may get people into compliance, but they will never inspire the extra level of intensity and dedication that creates excellence.

> **Strict financial controls may get people into compliance, but they will never inspire the extra level of intensity and dedication that creates excellence.**

While "having fun" can have many possible meanings, there is a difference between "happiness" and "contentment." True professionals commit themselves to the pursuit of happiness, and do not allow themselves to lapse into self-satisfied contentment. Professionals and professional firms can restore the fun (and morale and enthusiasm) by committing themselves to a path of true excellence and strict adherence to the highest values. This path will result in greater professional accomplishment, and the (superior) profits and satisfaction that flow from it.

To accomplish this, individuals and firms must recognize that there is a difference between "espoused values" (what they say they believe in) and "values-in-action" (how they actually live their professional lives). (The terms are borrowed from Chris Argyris.) This book is about trying to align professionals' real-world actions with their true (espoused) values.

In practice, what this means is that individuals and firms must rethink what they manage, measure, and discuss. If you value something, then you must monitor your performance in that area, accept nothing less than excellence, and actively work to learn what to do differently every time you fall short of excellence. Firms must provide help and counsel to those who are encountering difficulties in living up to their standards, in order to help them get back on track. Phrased another way, professionals have to decide on which subjects they are prepared to give "nagging rights." Professionals are used to being nagged about their production levels. Yet they are rarely nagged about such areas as levels of client service, supervision of junior professionals, or collaboration with each other.

Once professionals have confirmed their core values, they need to design systems which provide "consequences for noncompliance." By leaving each individual professional to decide for himself or herself what level to achieve in key value areas, firms are in effect saying that the firm, as a society, has no standards that *must* be adhered to. Excellence in these areas becomes a matter of personal professional choice. This is insufficient if firms are to live up to their values and reap the benefits that flow from the accomplishment of excellence.

"Consequences for noncompliance" need not be, and should not be, punitive. Professionals must live by the slogan "You're allowed to fail, you're not allowed to not try." If someone is exhibiting difficulties in achieving excellence in teamwork or project supervision or client service (or any of the firm's other core values), this needs to evoke a response from the firm which is characterized by concern, support, assistance, counseling, and everything else possible to help that person become aligned with the firm's values.

> **"Consequences for noncompliance" need not be, and should not be, punitive. Professionals must live by the slogan "You're allowed to fail, you're not allowed to not try."**

Doing this will require a special form of management. It will require managers (or leaders, or coaches) who are close enough to know what is going on in their groups so that they can quickly detect when there is noncompliance with firm values. These managers/leaders/coaches must also have the desire, the skills and the time to help other partners improve in areas that are valued.

It is the combination of enforced, common, agreed-upon values, together with the existence of helpful coaches, that will restore teamwork to a professional firm. It is the combination of enforced, common, agreed-upon values, together with the existence of helpful coaches, that will restore teamwork to a professional firm. Common goals and common values define a team. By selecting a few coaches willing to serve their colleagues by accepting responsibility for collective results, firms are more likely to ensure that they live by shared values.

None of this is about new compensation schemes. The primary mechanisms I propose are new measures (to monitor performance in new areas), and new forms of management (to provide feedback, guidance, and support). It is not effective in trying to preserve a value to say "If you don't do well according to our values, we'll just pay you less, and allow you to carry on in the same way."

If all these fail to get a particular professional aligned with a firm's values, then, yes, ultimately a compensation adjustment may be required. Compensation adjustment for a professional who performs poorly according to values should exist as a second-order consequence. "Exit" may in an extreme case have to be a third-order consequence for a professional who continually fails, over a long period of time, to live by a firm's values. However, both compensation adjustments and exit are signs of failure of the core system: sincere efforts by all professionals, supported by their colleagues, to live up to the highest standards in the areas they value.

As noted, the task is not only to clarify and establish values, but find mechanisms to enforce them. Based on ideas contained in this book and in *Managing the Professional Service Firm,* I often propose the following package to enforce values:

1. *Professionals agree to be coached and managed to strictly enforced, agreed-upon standards.* Appoint team leaders who are judged *solely* on the performance of the team, with their own personal statis-

tics being deemed irrelevant. A team leader's job is to *coach* team members, and to act as a primary agent for introducing consequences for noncompliance with excellence standards. Preferably, these consequences should consist of help, support, encouragement, and concern.

2. *Teamwork is mandatory, not optional.* Require every professional to belong to a team, "donating" a minimum number of nonbillable hours to the team, jointly scheduled by the team, with strict accountability for projects committed to.

3. *Continual investment must be made in getting better.* Every team submits a quarterly nonbillable hour budget showing which actions will be taken in the areas of (a) generating better business, not just more business; (b) lowering the cost to the firm of performing selected professional tasks; (c) becoming more valuable to clients on current tasks; and (d) disseminating skills, horizontally and vertically.

4. *Enforce excellence in wise management of clients' resources and firm's finances.* Measure and track profitability at the engagement level, thereby holding professionals accountable for the profitability of their matters (revenues and costs), not just personal billable hours.

5. *Excellence in client satisfaction is an enforced standard.* Institute mandatory client feedback on every transaction, with full managerial follow-up, with results to be used in performance counseling and compensation. Eventually, the firm should offer an unconditional satisfaction guarantee.

6. *Excellence in managing those you supervise is an enforced professional standard.* Institute mandatory "upward feedback" on project supervision performance for every transaction, to enforce good supervision of matters, with strict accountability for results.

7. *Personal professional growth is a nonnegotiable minimum standard.* Require every professional to demonstrate personal professional/career progress every year (zero tolerance for cruising).

Personal progress on a personal strategic plan is a strict accountability.

8. *All partners must show a sincere interest in clients' affairs and a sincere desire to help them.* Require all professionals to demonstrate an understanding of their client's business and thereby contribute to business development.

9. *Departmental resources are considered collective assets and cannot be allocated autonomously.* The team leader is responsible for staffing all engagements; no professional has the autonomy to staff his or her own job.

10. *Primary focus must be on relationship building.* Allocate specific nonbillable budgets to be spent nurturing designated key existing clients, the total of these budgets to sum at least 60% of all nonbillable marketing hours.

11. *Be intolerant about the pursuit of excellence.* Be prepared to fire any professional who does not participate in these programs. "You're allowed to fail; you're not allowed to not try!"

I don't believe that this is the *only* possible package. Some individuals and firms will substitute different values and different enforcement mechanisms. But, if they are to achieve excellence, the values must be clear and the enforcement mechanisms real.

Summary

Little of this is new. Tom Peters once quoted Ray Kroc, the founder of McDonald's, to the effect that, to succeed at McDonald's, "You must be able to see the beauty in a hamburger bun." Most so-called "sophisticated" professionals laugh when they hear this, but just a few moments of reflection should make it clear that Mr. Kroc was right. You can't become the world leader in a business as basic as hamburgers (or any other) without truly caring, passionately, about what you do. A more recent work, *Built to Last,* by James Collins and Jerry Porras, supports this point. They show that truly visionary (and successful) companies have discovered that there is no conflict between the pursuit of profit and having a purpose beyond profit.

The lesson is clear: Believe passionately in what you do, and never knowingly compromise your standards and values. Act like a true professional, aiming for true excellence, and the money will follow. Act like a prostitute, with an attitude of "I'll do it for the money, but don't expect me to care," and you'll lose the premium that excellence earns. True professionalism wins!

> **Believe passionately in what you do, and never knowingly compromise your standards and values. Act like a true professional, aiming for true excellence, and the money will follow.**

Part One

(MOSTLY)
ABOUT YOU

1

REAL PROFESSIONALISM

I frequently ask professionals what they consider to be the difference between a good secretary and a great secretary. The answers flow freely. Great secretaries, I am told:

- Take pride in their work, and show a personal commitment to quality
- Reach out for responsibility
- Anticipate, and don't wait to be told what to do—they show initiative
- Do whatever it takes to get the job done
- Get involved and don't just stick to their assigned role
- Are always looking for ways to make things easier for those they serve
- Are eager to learn as much as they can about the business of those they serve
- Really listen to the needs of those they serve
- Learn to understand and think like those they serve so they can represent them when they are not there

- Are team players
- Can be trusted with confidences
- Are honest, trustworthy, and loyal
- Are open to constructive critiques on how to improve

All of this list can be summarized in one phrase: Great secretaries *care.*

Two obvious points need to be made about this list. First and foremost, it is applicable to all of us, not just to secretaries. With virtually no modifications, this list could serve to delineate the defining characteristics of what differentiates a great consultant from a good one, a great lawyer from a good one, and so on. Indeed, this list is a reasonable *definition* of what it means to be a professional.

Second, this list has nothing to do with technical skills. Few secretaries are deemed to be "great" because of their ability to type 95 words a minute or file documents in nanoseconds. Similarly, very few professionals become known by their clients as "great" purely as a result of technical abilities. The opposite of the word *professional* is not *unprofessional,* but rather *technician.*

Technicians may be highly skilled, but they aren't professionals until they reliably and consistently demonstrate the characteristics listed above. Professionalism is predominantly an attitude, not a set of competencies. A real professional is a technician who cares. (You may recall the old slogan "People don't care how much you know until they know how much you care.")

> **Professionalism is predominantly an attitude, not a set of competencies. A real professional is a technician who cares.**

How many of us so-called professionals are prepared to be held accountable for behaving according to the standards set by this list? Yet we often ask people who earn a fraction of what professionals earn to meet these standards. This raises an interesting question: Why would secretaries be willing to strive for such standards? Why would anyone who *isn't* sharing the profits want to demonstrate this level of commitment?

To find out, I asked Julie O'Leary, who began in 1985 as my secretary and who is now my business manager. Julie meets and exceeds every one of the standards listed above. This is what she had to say:

> Professional is not a label you give yourself—it's a description you hope others will apply to you. You do the best you can as a matter of self-respect. Having self-respect is the key to earning respect and trust from others. If you want to be trusted and respected you have to earn it. These behaviors lead to job fulfillment. The question should really be, "Why wouldn't someone want to do this?" If someone takes a job, or starts a career worrying about what's in it for them, looking to do just enough to get by, or being purely self-serving in their performance—they will go nowhere. Even if they manage to excel through the ranks as good technicians—they will not be happy in what they are doing. The work will be boring, aggravating, tiresome, and a drag.

Professional is not a label you give yourself—it's a description you hope others will apply to you.

It should be clear from this why I consider Julie O'Leary to be more of a professional than many of the lawyers, consultants, accountants, engineers, and actuaries that I meet. (I sometimes worry that her professional standards exceed my own.) If you've ever been a purchaser of a professional service, or an employer, you'll probably agree that finding people with technical skill is usually easy, but finding people who behave consistently in the ways described above is hard. It is rare to find individuals (and even harder to find whole firms) filled with the energy, drive, and enthusiasm, as well as the personal commitment to excellence, that Julie has shown. Why is this?

Traditional Views of Professionalism

Part of the problem, I believe, lies in what people believe professionalism to be. As we have seen, *real* professionalism has little, if anything, to do with which business you are in, what role within that business you perform, or how many degrees you have. Rather, it implies a pride in work, a commitment to quality, a dedication to the interests of the client, and a sincere desire to help.

However, traditional definitions of professionalism are filled with references to status, educational attainments, "noble" callings, and things like the right of practitioners to autonomy—the privilege of practicing free of direction. All of these definitions are self-interested. (As George Bernard Shaw suggested, "All professions are conspiracies against the laity.")

Perhaps one reason for the scarcity of real professionalism may be that the recruiting process in professional firms is flawed. Real professionalism is about *attitudes,* and perhaps even about *character.* Yet few firms screen very effectively for this in their hiring, either at entry level or when bringing in more-experienced, lateral-entry hires. Most hiring processes are about educational qualifications and technical skills.

As Julie once pointed out: "Firms should hire for attitude, and train for skill. Skills you can teach—attitudes and character are inherent. They can be suppressed or encouraged to develop, but they have to be there to begin with."

"Firms should hire for attitude, and train for skill. Skills you can teach—attitudes and character are inherent."

Another of my favorite discussion questions is to ask people "Why do you do what you do?" Obviously things like money, meaning, and intellectual challenge are important, but the one I always listen for is "I like helping people." If that one is missing, I know I am speaking with a professional in trouble.

Too many professionals don't do what they do because they want to help their clients; they're in it only for the money or the personal prestige. In my view, such professionals may become good, and even earn good incomes, but they will never be considered great.

In recent years, many firms have debated the question "Are we a profession or are we a business?" I have found many of these debates to be misconceived. Many of those who argue that they are a business say that they cannot afford the laissez-faire management approaches of the past, and must focus more on financial realities. In reply, those who have argued that they are a profession appeal to the needs for autonomy, professional fulfillment, and freedom from bureaucratic constraints. In my view, *both* sides are wrong.

Being a professional is neither about money nor about professional fulfillment. Both of these are consequences of an unqualified dedication to excellence in serving clients and their needs. As Dale Carnegie wrote many years ago: "You'll have more fun and success helping other people achieve *their* goals than you will trying to reach your own goals."

A related problem may be how people are being "socialized" into the professions by schools and by firms—I suspect that many truly don't understand what professional life is really all about. For example, in recent years I have seen many so-called professionals undergo a form of status shock. An acquaintance of mine, a top-of-the-class MBA type, recently left the consulting profession after many years with a top-tier firm because, as he said: "In the early years clients gave me respect because I solved their problems, but now I'm treated like a vendor. They question my recommendations, make me justify everything I plan to do on their behalf, and watch my spending like a hawk. I'm not used to being in the subservient role, and I don't like it."

This acquaintance was (and is) entirely accurate about how significant the changes have been in how clients deal with professionals. In the past, professionals were often given respect and trust automatically because of their position. That's no longer true. However, what this person failed to understand (or to accept) is that it is still possible to be treated with respect and trust—but now you really have to *earn* and *deserve* these things. None of this should be a surprise; as Bob Dylan once wrote, "You Gotta Serve Somebody."

Perhaps it is time for our schools and professional firms alike to stop teaching students that they are the best and the brightest, the special elite in the noblest profession of all (whatever that profession happens to be). Maybe schools and firms should find ways to teach more about what it is to serve a client, and about how to work with people whether they be your juniors, your seniors, or your colleagues. (When I talk with business-school alumni about their careers

> Being a professional is neither about money nor about professional fulfillment. Both of these are consequences of an unqualified dedication to excellence in serving clients and their needs.

and what they would have done differently to prepare for them, the most common reply is "I wish I had paid more attention to the courses about dealing with people.")

It's Not (Just) About the Money

If you review the preceding list of behaviors (commitment to quality, reaching out for responsibility, doing what it takes to get the job done, etc.), it should be obvious that people who exhibited these behaviors would be on a fast-track path to economic success. As Julie pointed out, it is doing these things that earn you respect and trust, whether from colleagues or clients. If this is true—that professionalism *works*—then why don't more people operate this way?

I have frequently posed this question to groups ranging from senior professionals to secretaries. I must report that the most common reply I hear is "Well, I'm not compensated for doing all that." This is of course a Catch-22. In most organizations, you *would* be rewarded (eventually) if you behaved this way. But if you wait to be rewarded *before* you do it, then you'll probably wait forever. The problem, then, is that people may be too short-term in their thinking—they are focusing on their jobs, not their careers. The noble path *does* win, but only if you are prepared to make the investment to act professionally over a long period of time.

The noble path *does* win, but only if you are prepared to make the investment to act professionally over a long period of time.

Another factor that suppresses people's desire to act professionally (at least in the terms in which I have defined it) is the environment in which they work—how they are managed. It is easier to find the discipline and motivation to behave professionally if everyone around you is doing the same. However, I am frequently told that this is not the case. I often hear comments like "Why should I strive for excellence when everyone else is just doing enough to get by? I'd be willing to participate if everyone else was behaving this way, but it gets pretty demotivating to be the only one really trying with nobody noticing."

What this comment points out is that even if you have a firm filled with people who have the attitude and character to be real professionals, it is all too easy to fall into the trap of creating an environment that demotivates them. If those at the top are not living, breathing exemplars of real professionalism, it is easy for those lower down to conclude that commitment and professionalism are not required "around here."

So what is it that encourages people to act professionally, and also creates the environment that allows real professionals to flourish? The answers are as old as the hills, even if they are just as frequently forgotten. Here's Julie's advice again:

• "Remember to show appreciation to the one who has taken that extra step or surprised you with an exceptional performance. This will breed more enthusiasm and more good work.

• "Don't be afraid to give people ever more responsible assignments (trust them), and if it doesn't come out perfect, let them try again after you've given them some pointers. Everyone likes a challenge.

• "Get people involved. Share reports, conversations, information about competitors and clients, etc., so that everyone can see the big picture and how they fit into it.

• "Constructive critiques are one of the most powerful learning tools available to the employee. Take the time to help people learn—not as a matter of performance appraisal, nor an issue of compensation, but simply as a sincere desire to help them improve.

• "Don't promote teamwork and then only recognize the captain. Make sure recognition is given to everyone in some way. It doesn't have to be money—it can be as simple as saying 'Well done.' Take a friend to lunch—'It's on me.' Work hard to make people feel part of what's going on."

To Julie's comments, I'd add a few of my own. I believe that *everyone* likes to feel that what you're doing has a purpose—that you're doing something meaningful in the world. If all anyone ever talks about is the money, it gets pretty depressing. You can't just pay people to be dedicated, motivated professionals. You must reward them if they are, but money alone won't do it. Ultimately, you must *inspire* them to be as professional as they know how to be. To get people to be professionals, you must treat them as professionals—and be tolerant of nothing less.

To get people to be professionals, you must treat them as professionals—and be tolerant of nothing less.

Julie's view on this is as follows: "If the person has the right character, and you treat them as you would want to be treated, they will respond with enthusiasm and commitment. If they don't, then you should reassess what the person is doing working for you. Or maybe they need to reassess if they're in the right job."

I hope these thoughts cause the reader, whether a managing partner or a secretary, to ponder two questions that we all need to think about frequently. First: Do other people consider me a professional? (How well do those I serve think I meet the criteria on page one?) Second: Do I deal with those who work for me in such a way as to encourage their commitment and professionalism, or do I sometimes act to suppress it? (How good am I at bringing out the professionalism in others?)

2

ARE YOU HAVING FUN YET?

Professional success requires more than talent. Among other things, it requires drive, initiative, commitment, involvement, and—above all—enthusiasm. Yet these things are often missing from professionals' lives. Consider the following quiz.

Think back on all the work you have done in the past year or so, and divide it among three categories, the first of which is "God, I love this! *This* is why I do what I do!" The second category is "It's OK, I can tolerate it—it's what I do for a living." The third category is "I hate this part—I wish I could get rid of this junk!" Before reading on, estimate your answers to this question.

Figured it out? Then let me report the results of putting this question to top professionals in prestige firms around the world. The typical answers I am given are 20% to 25% for "God, I love this!"; 60% to 70% for "I can tolerate it"; and 5% to 20% for "I hate this part." In other words, the typical professional in a top firm is positively enjoying his or her work about one day a week.

Now, a second question: Think about all the clients you have served in the past year and, again, divide them into three categories. Category

1 is "I like these people, and their industry interests me." (Yes, I know I'm combining two things.) Category 2 is "I can tolerate these people and their business is OK—neither fascinating nor boring." Category 3 is "I'm professional enough that I would never say this to them, and I'll still do my best for them, but the truth is that these are not my kind of people, and I have no interest in their industry."

Ready to compare results? Typical answers from top professionals around the world are 30% to 35% for "I like these people"; 50% to 60% for "I can tolerate these people"; and 5% to 20% for "These are not my kind of people." (I must stress that these are *not* my opinions about professional life, but what individuals in top-drawer firms tell me about their work lives.)

These estimates provide the single biggest reason to reintroduce some energy into your professional life. Why spend the majority of that life working on *tolerable* stuff for *acceptable* clients when, with some effort in (for example) client relations, marketing, and selling, you can spend your days working on *exciting* things for *interesting* people?

More than money, more than volume, more in fact than anything else, an individual professional should be involved in marketing for one reason above all: The better you are at marketing, the better the chance you have to work on fun stuff, and the less trapped you become in being forced to take on work and clients you don't truly enjoy, simply to "feed the baby."

The better you are at marketing, the better the chance you have to work on fun stuff, and the less trapped you become in being forced to take on work and clients you don't truly enjoy.

However, I must report that a common reaction among professionals to the percentages given above is to think that those numbers are inevitable (i.e., that they accurately measure how much excitement professional life has to offer). "Most of professional work *is* routine and most of the clients *are* uninteresting," I'm told. My reaction is "I'll readily concede that there's boring work for dull clients out there, but the question is 'Why do *you* have to do it?'" The next sentence I hear is "But do I have a choice?"

The answer is "Of course you do!" Unless you dislike *all* clients and *all* of their matters (in which case you should reconsider your chosen profession), we are only talking about exercising some discretion and energy in influencing what you work on. Supposedly, professionals are among society's most bright, educated, and elite members—people who are supposed to have more career choices than anyone else. Yet they seem to be willing to accept a work life made up largely of "I can tolerate it" work and clients, and they feel that they cannot safely do anything about all that.

At one of the most profitable, elite law firms in the United States, I started to pose my questions, asking "What percent of your clients would you put in the category of 'I like these people?'" The room broke into laughter, as if the question was absurd. It became clear that many professionals do not *expect* to like their clients. The issue here is not an ethical or moral one (that you *should* like your clients and your work), but rather that it *is possible* to like (some of) them; and further that it is within every professional's power to influence which clients you work for, and what you do for them.

Fred Bartlit, an eminent American lawyer, has enumerated the reasons why professional life *should be* the most exciting career there is. (This quote was taken from a comment posted on Counsel Connect, an online computer service for lawyers.)

> Professionals [he said "lawyers"] are interesting, smart people who are interesting to spend time with. The problems we face are fascinating and are different almost every day. We learn about many different businesses. We deal with many different clients. We are not stuck in a rut of having the same boss for 10 years. Because we deal with ideas, one person can make a difference. We deal with cutting-edge issues. As professionals, we do not have "bosses." We work for ourselves and have only ourselves to satisfy. We have a lot of personal freedom. We do not have to be in a particular place every day at a particular time. Finally, we are well paid compared to most executives. The [professions], then, should be a terrific way to spend time. We work in small groups of highly motivated, interesting people, addressing ever-changing, complex problems where there is a lot at stake. What could be better?

It could be argued that in spite of this potential for fun, excitement, and fulfillment, it is firm management policies that induce the dissatisfaction (and lethargy) previously described. In too many firms, the only relevant measurement criterion is how busy you are (measured in billable hours or personal billings), and considerations of whether one actually enjoys one's work is irrelevant at best. Time-based billing causes individuals (and firms) to focus on the quantity of work, and not at all on its caliber. Similarly, many firms' approach to marketing is nondiscriminating ("All new revenue is good revenue"), leading to an environment wherein considerations of current cash overwhelm issues of professional fulfillment.

Perverse, dysfunctional, short-term firm systems exist, but are beside the point. Yes, the firm's management and culture may be to blame, but waiting for the firm to change before *you* change is only to cheat yourself. Why don't more people reach out, take control of their own business development, and get *both* benefits—cash *and* fun?

> **The firm's management and culture may be to blame, but waiting for the firm to change before *you* change is only to cheat yourself.**

Done right, there is *not* a trade-off here for the individual. You'll stay just as busy and make as much money (probably more) working on exciting stuff for clients you like as you will on the dull stuff for uninteresting clients—and *any* firm would reward that just as highly. The virtuous circle even extends to marketing itself. You'll be more successful marketing to clients you like, on issues that interest you, than you will be trying to market to clients you don't care for, on stuff you can barely tolerate. So firm pressure to "stay billable" does not, in my view, explain the situation.

Clearly there is some sense of helplessness, as if the situation were inevitable. Many professionals seem to have given up on the dream that professional life can be fulfilling. In discussing this topic, I have heard many times the phrase "It's a job—what more can you expect?" For me, this choice of phrase is telling. In trying to explain what makes professional life different from other (e.g., corporate) walks of life, I have always asserted that while others may seek *jobs,* the defining characteristic of professionals is that they seek *careers.*

Evidently my assumption is false, at least as far as many professionals are concerned. Perhaps there was a time, maybe when they were trying to make partner, when they thought of what they did as a career. But now? Apparently they have settled into the "It's a job" mode. I have been explicitly told by many good and smart professionals that they do not *expect* to find passion in their work lives. Their fulfillment comes from their families, their hobbies, and/or their home lives. They no longer expect to find it at work.

> You'll be more successful marketing to clients you like, on issues that interest you, than you will be trying to market to clients you don't care for, on stuff you can barely tolerate.

Many are the victims of their own past success. There exists in many large firms a Lost Generation of (mostly younger) professionals who became partners by keeping their heads down, putting in vast numbers of billable hours on work generated by others, abdicating control over their own work lives to "the machine," and never being required to demonstrate individual initiative. Nonpartner life in most large professional firms often breeds a helpless sense of lack of personal control over one's work life, and it is therefore not surprising that, upon reaching partner status, many find the concept of choice and personal control a foreign notion.

Still I am surprised. The attitude of many I meet is "Why should I even try? Business development efforts are risky and time-consuming, and my firm doesn't support or reward efforts, only successes. And since I'm rewarded primarily for hours, that's what I focus on!" To me, such sentiments reflect a mentality as shortsighted and perverse as the firm's. *Of course* the firm needs to change, but if you wait for that you'll wait till hell freezes over, and meanwhile *you* live a less fulfilling life. To me, this reflects an abdication of responsibility for one's own future.

For many, part of the paralysis that I observe derives from a profound misunderstanding of what business development is truly about. Leaning on the caricature of business development as "encyclopedia selling," many believe that "I don't have rainmaking skills." This is

Being good at business development involves nothing more than a sincere interest in clients and their problems, and a willingness to go out and spend the time being helpful to them.

nonsense. Being good at business development involves nothing more than a sincere interest in clients and their problems, and a willingness to go out and spend the time being helpful to them. (See Chapter 17, "How Real Professionals Develop Business.")

If you really *are* interested in a (particular type of) client, and clearly demonstrate both your ability and your willingness to help them, getting hired has no magic to it. The biggest trouble for many professionals is that they haven't taken the time to figure out which clients they like. You don't have to like *every* client—indeed, that's the whole point, since you can't. Hence the need arises to decide on whom you *do* like, and to structure a plan to get more of their work, and the work of clients similar to them.

There can be no denying that achieving a high percentage of "God, I love this!" work means that one needs to reflect on what one loves and why. I observe frequently that many professionals are undergoing status shock. They thought they were joining an elite, intellectually driven profession where they would be treated by clients as gurus. They then discover that they are treated as vendors with no special rank or privilege. Professional schools attract many people who want to avoid commercial life and then find themselves thrust straight into it—and of course disliking it. They do it anyway to earn a living, but their value systems are such that they think they should be doing something more "noble." They were attracted to the prestige and money of professional life, but don't actually like what getting it involves.

In such cases, I am reminded of the song lyric by Steve Stills which recommends that if you can't be with the one you love, you should love the one you're with. Part of the art of achieving a fulfilling work life is always seeking the angle that makes it a challenge, the view of it that makes it fun. Loving what you do is less an inherent characteristic of the work itself and more a reflection of the frame of mind you bring to your tasks.

Where does all this leave us? With a simple but powerful conclusion: The missing element in most professionals' lives is the most important. They often already have money, prestige, title, and standing. What they *don't* have is fun.

> The missing element in most professionals' lives is the most important. They often already have money, prestige, title, and standing. What they *don't* have is fun.

When one reviews who is successful (and thus happy) among professionals, it quickly emerges that it has nothing to do with IQ, where you went to school, or what training you received. Those who succeed are those who can recapture the magic and excitement they felt when they were first setting out to build a career, and were willing to work hard to make it happen. All it takes to find the fun is a little energy, ambition, drive, and enthusiasm. So scarce are these characteristics that they are today the dominant competitive advantage for both individual professionals and firms.

Enthusiasm and involvement are the keys, and yes, you can do something about your life. You are not powerless. Remember, the point of life is to be happy. All other goals (money, fame, status, responsibility, achievement) are merely ways of making you happy. They are worthless in themselves.

3

NO REGRETS

I will never forget the best piece of career advice I ever received. I was a young assistant professor at the Harvard Business School, eager to figure out what I had to do to get tenure (i.e., "make partner"). I went to one of the elder statesmen of the school to find out what was required of me.

"You're asking the wrong question, David," he said. "The rule here is very simple. If the rest of the world wants you, we'll probably want you. If the rest of the world doesn't want you, we probably won't want you. Focus on being the best you can be at what you want to do."

At the time, I thought this answer was evasive and unsatisfactory. "But what should I focus on?" I asked. "Should I choose a functional discipline, an industry specialty, or something else?" "It's up to you" he replied. "Do whatever you enjoy. Don't choose something you don't enjoy just because you think it's what we want."

Somewhat skeptically, I followed his advice, and it led me, many years later, to the point where I chose a consulting career (which I love and which has flourished) rather than pursuing an academic one. I enjoyed every minute I was in academia, and I've enjoyed every minute since I left. I have no regrets—it's been fun all the way.

As the decades have passed, I have come to realize the profound wisdom of my mentor's remarks. The message is simple: Success comes from doing what you enjoy. If you don't enjoy it, how can it be called *success*?

> **Success comes from doing what you enjoy. If you don't enjoy it, how can it be called *success*?**

The Power of Passion

Many people approach their career (or business) planning as an analytical exercise about which markets are growing and which services are in demand. While this is relevant data, I believe that career (or business) planning is not primarily an analytical task. In predicting professional success, enthusiasm and passion (and the hard work they inspire) count for much more than an extra piece of ability.

In my observations of professionals it is perfectly clear that success does not necessarily come to those with the highest IQ, or those who went to the best schools, or even those who chose the most popular specialty. Rather, lifelong drive and determination have been more influential in predicting professional success. Unless you are working at something you love, it is hard to find the discipline to exhibit drive and determination.

This thought is not new. Frequently cited is a quote from U.S. President Calvin Coolidge: "Nothing in the world can take the place of persistence. Talent will not; nothing is more common than unsuccessful men with talent. Genius will not; unrewarded genius is almost a proverb. Education will not; the world is full of educated derelicts. Persistence and determination alone are omnipotent."

Many people, when making career plans, ask themselves what they are good at. However, as Coolidge pointed out, talents (or skills or strengths) are not the key issue, even if they are relevant. Rather, what is important is what inspires persistence and determination—in other words, what you *care* about. Don't worry about what you're good at.

If something turns you on, you'll be good enough. If it doesn't, you won't. Your strengths are irrelevant: What you *like* is critical.

Figuring Out What You Want

This simple message is often ignored, particularly by professionals in midcareer who have attained partner status (or its equivalent). Many are not working at things they enjoy, and—worse—many have not taken the time to figure out how they *could* make their work life more fulfilling. While they may have annual goals, budgets, and performance reports, few professionals have a ready answer to questions such as these:

- What do you want to do next?
- Where would you like to be three years from now?
- What kind of clients would you like to have in three years?
- What kind of work would you like to be doing in three years?
- What next career challenge would you find most exciting?

These questions represent nothing more than having a continuously updated and revised personal strategic plan for your career. They are not about things that you do to meet *your firm's* needs and goals. This is about *you,* and *your* professional satisfaction. The questions are intended to force to the surface the essential issue that every one of us must address: Where am I going (next) in my career?

Many professionals are too busy worrying about their firm's performance criteria to figure out what success really means to them. They don't take the time to ask "What do I really want to accomplish during the next stage of my career? What would truly satisfy me?"

Many professionals are too busy worrying about their firm's performance criteria to figure out what success really means to them.

Many people do not know what career options they have. They don't know what it is that they could love, and don't know how to figure out what kind of professional practice would engage their enthusiasms. They truly don't know what they want. I am frequently asked "How do I figure out what I want?"

There is no perfect recipe; but here are a few things I think I've learned by watching thousands of professionals in action over the past 15 years.

The Recent Past

The obvious way to start is by reflecting on the past few years of your practice, and asking yourself "When did I have the most fun?"

I recommend that you pull out (or create) a list of every assignment you've done in the past three years, and question yourself. On which assignments, and with which clients, did you most enjoy working? When did you feel most fulfilled? When did you impress yourself, or otherwise feel most proud of yourself? ("Wow, did I do that?") If you can answer these questions, you are well on the way to a personal strategic plan—all you have to do is figure out how to get more of those kinds of assignments and/or those kinds of clients.

These questions may be obvious, but few professionals actually take the time to look back on their practice and consider these issues.

With Whom Do You Want to Deal?

More than any other factor, it is the people we have to deal with that determine the quality of our work lives. Since the overwhelming majority of professional and business life is spent dealing with people—clients, colleagues, subordinates, and superiors—you'll be happier if you like and respect the people with whom you'll be doing business. Do you know whom you like and respect most? Construct a career that will allow you to spend the majority of your time with those you especially like and respect. Life's too short to spend it dealing with idiots. As philosopher Jean-Paul Sartre noted, "Hell is other people."

Most of us want not only to respect those we deal with, but also to *be* respected and appreciated. Accordingly, you should ask yourself "Whom do I want to impress—whose approval do I want to win?" You can't impress everyone simultaneously. Different people are impressed by different things: money, status, intellect, interpersonal skills, character, contributions to society, and so on. Ask yourself "For what do I want to be admired, and by whom?"

We *all* want to impress people. The tough part is figuring out precisely whom we want to impress, and why. Similarly, we *all* want respect and prestige. But in whose eyes? It is more likely that you'll find the right answer by thinking about the clients you want to impress and the people you want to serve. If you accomplish that, impressing colleagues and co-workers will take care of itself. Your colleagues, like my mentor at the Harvard Business School, will be most impressed if you do something that the *outside* world acknowledges.

Evil Secrets

The following exercise may help you to clarify what you *really* want. One way to discover what you truly like or love is to ask yourself what the things are that you *don't* like to admit. Suppose you say "I don't like to admit it, but I need to be the center of attention." OK, then find a career path that will let you show off. If you say "I don't like to admit it, but I don't like dealing with other people." Well, then devise a role that will let you make your contribution through things done at the office, such as intellectual creativity and true technical superiority. Should you say "I don't like to admit it, but I really want to be rich." Fine, then go out and build a business. Perhaps you even feel forced to say "I don't like to admit it, but I'm an intellectual snob." All right, then find a career path that will allow you to work only with smart people.

Play *to* your "evil secrets." Don't suppress them. You are a lot less flexible than you think.

Play *to* your "evil secrets." Don't suppress them. You are a lot less flexible than you think.

Planning Horizons

One of the reasons many professionals do not love what they currently do is that they have outgrown it. They *used to* find what they do challenging and exciting, but they've done it too many times now to still feel the thrill. There is a lesson here: Don't think too far ahead!

Few career choices are forever. The choice to be made is not what you want to do with your entire career, but which *next* challenge would fulfill you (over say a three-year period). Most successful professionals I know have had varied careers, with a pattern of sequential specializations. At any one time they were completely absorbed in something, but after a while they moved on to something else.

> Few career choices are forever. The choice to be made is not what you want to do with your entire career, but which *next* challenge would fulfill you.

Many successful careers, when viewed retrospectively, look like an eminently logical progression, as if a single career choice was made and laid out at the beginning. Few of them really were planned that way. Careers are built by moving from one challenge to the next. Successful professionals don't focus on where they want to end up ultimately—few of us are that prescient. Rather, they focus on what they're going to do *next*.

Don't try to plan *too* far ahead. In 5 to 10 years you'll be a different person who wants different things from life. (How many of us have the same goals today that we did 10 years ago?) Choose something that will be exciting and challenging, and will make you happy for maybe the next few years. The longer term will take care of itself.

The Advice of Others

No one else can tell you what you *should* want in your career. In fact, my advice is to ban the word "should" from your career planning. There are usually a lot of people around you—colleagues, superiors, loved ones, and friends—who will tell you what you should want from your career (and from life in general), especially if you ask them. It is *fatal* to be overly influenced by them!

Those around you can help by providing options, ideas, suggestions, or market and business opportunities that they think would be best for you. It's always a good idea to solicit outside opinions, in order to expand the range of alternatives to be considered. But you *don't* have to accept other people's ideas and conclusions, even if what you hear has a common theme. Don't get stampeded by what people around you value. The task is to figure out what *you* value—and value highly enough to throw yourself into with unqualified passion.

Don't Sell: Buy!

As you plan the next phase of your career, bear in mind that happiness in professional life is determined much more by the role you play (the tasks you perform, the people you deal with) than by which firm you're with or profession you're in. Many people choose a profession, then a firm, and finally a role. I believe this is the wrong order. Figure out which role you want to play, and then (if necessary) tell your firm about your decision. If they don't accept it, change firms. Don't sell: Buy!

If you are thinking of a new role, ask yourself what you really need to know about the career choice you have selected in order to be sure you'll be happy. Find someone who's already doing what you're thinking of doing. Don't be afraid to seek him or her out and ask questions. Check it out. Don't sell: Buy!

Remember, planning your career is up to you, *not* your firm. If your new career path doesn't work out, the results will be a lot more painful for you than for your firm. Remember, planning your career is up to you, *not* your firm. If your new career path doesn't work out, the results will be a lot more painful for you than for your firm. You should be a lot pickier than they in deciding what you're going to do. Don't sell: Buy!

In my experience, I've seen many professionals fail to develop the sort of plans described here—because they feel relatively powerless. "After all," they say, "it's a tough market out there, and I can't afford to work only on what I like. I have to work at what I can get." In many ways, comments like this prove my point. Nothing is more impressive (and hence marketable) than someone who clearly knows what he or she loves, and why. Someone *without* a passionate commitment to a practice will indeed have to take whatever is available. You can either buy yourself a career, or be bought by one. Don't sell: Buy!

4

DYNAMOS, CRUISERS, AND LOSERS

At any given stage in your professional life, your performance can be that of a Dynamo, a Cruiser, or a Loser. In which category are you currently?

You are a Dynamo when you are acting as if you are still in the middle of a career (not a job) and on your way to somewhere. As a Dynamo, you always have a personal strategic plan that you are enthusiastically working towards fulfilling. Dynamos are always working to learn something new, and are continually adding to their skills and knowledge. They are actively building their practice in new and challenging areas.

> **Dynamos are always working to learn something new, and are continually adding to their skills and knowledge.**

Dynamos are vigorous in finding ways to get out of the flow of repetitive work (giving away their "overly familiar" client work to others in the firm) even if they are superb at it. Their view is: "Although I may be the most skilled person around here at this task, I've done it too many times. I need to find someone else to do it—without compromising my clients' interests—so that I can move on to more challenging, exciting things!"

Being a Dynamo is not primarily about marketing and client development, although these may be required. Rather, it is about active career development and continuous self-improvement.

At the other extreme is the Loser. You are a Loser if, for whatever reason, you do not meet the basic standards of quality, client service, and hard work. This state, whether temporary or permanent, can be caused by any of many possible things: disruptions in one's personal life, a loss of energy, a dying practice area, and so on.

If you are in the middle category, that of the Cruiser, you are by definition, *not* a Loser. Cruisers are fully competent, successful professionals who work hard, do good work, and take care of their clients. They show up each week and "make the sausages." Then they come in the next week, and, again, make the sausages. Most likely theirs are good, high-quality "sausages." In fact, everybody in the firm knows that if you've got a sausage job, you should go to that person. Those people are terrific at making sausages! However, Cruisers certainly are not Dynamos. They are not *going* anywhere. Rather than working to learn new things, Cruisers do well for the time being by living off their existing skills. They are not working to expand their abilities. They have a job, *not* a career.

Note that being categorized as a Cruiser doesn't imply that one is a bad worker or a bad person. Quite the opposite: Cruising translates to dedicated, high-quality work. We *all* cruise *some* of the time; the temptation to do so is huge. Cruising means working at what you are already good at, and in consequence usually means a low-stress, comfortable work life. Furthermore, it is easier to get hired for what you already know how to do than it is to generate work that "moves you forward."

However, it is equally clear that a professional cannot cruise forever. If all you work on is what you already know how to do, you'll eventually be overtaken by someone younger who will learn how to do what you do, and will probably be willing to do it for less than you get paid. A key to success is to find a way to only cruise (if at all) occasionally and for short periods.

> **If all you work on is what you already know how to do, you'll eventually be overtaken by someone younger.**

In taking polls on this issue in a wide variety of firms worldwide, professionals report to me that they would place 10% to 20% of their colleagues in the Dynamo category, 5% to 15% in the Loser category, and fully 65% to 85% in the Currently Cruising group. (My preference is to ask people about where they think their *colleagues* are, rather than where they categorize *themselves*. Self-evaluations, I have learned, are more suspect than external perspectives!)

Many firms, particularly during weak economic times, think they have addressed their strategic issues by "tackling" unproductive professionals (turning some around, and firing the others). However, these estimated percentages suggest that the problem for most professional firms is not the number of Losers, but the much larger number of people who are doing fine right now, yet not really *growing* as professionals. Cruising on one's existing talents, rather than working to build upon them, appears to be commonplace in even the best of firms.

The strategic challenge for professional firms is clearly not one of which direction to point the thundering herd in. The simple fact is that the herd is not thundering! The problem to be solved is not that of market positioning, segmentation, value propositions, or competitive strategy. The first issue to be addressed is whether or not the Cruisers (often the majority of the professionals) have the energy or the appetite to strive for success levels beyond those they have already achieved.

One of the most common comments I hear among professionals is "We're already successful, so why do we have to change? We're not losers!" As far as it goes, this is correct—these professionals *are* successful. True, but irrelevant: The central issue for *all* professionals is not how successful you are now, but whether or not you are prepared to strive for *greater* success.

It is remarkable how scarce sustained ambition can be among those who have already achieved a degree of success. I often hear the comment "But surely we can't all be Dynamos? *Someone's* got to do the work!" This question misuses the term's definition. Being a Dynamo isn't about being a business-getter, leaving Cruisers to be those who

> **It is remarkable how scarce sustained ambition can be among those who have already achieved a degree of success.**

perform the professional tasks. This is a misunderstanding. A Dynamo is someone who is always learning, growing, and expanding their skills. *Everyone* can (and must) do this!

I remember very well the time that Julie (my business manager) came to me and said "David, I've been observing what our outside accountant has been doing in preparing our company's tax filings, and I think I could learn to do what he does. So, here's the deal. If you'll pay the fees for me to go to tax school at night, I'll donate the time to learn. That way, we'll only have to use the outside accountant for the advanced stuff. What do you think?"

What did I think? I thought what I *still* think—that Julie is a Dynamo! She is more of a Dynamo than many professional firm partners I know.

What Julie understands (and acts on) is the simple truth that if you're not learning new things, then you are becoming obsolete. Remember, every firm in your profession—including your own—is furiously training people to learn how to do what you do. Unless you justify your extra years of experience with additional skill, knowledge, and ability, you'll be overtaken. Cruising is not an option for anyone who wants to have a career five years from now!

How Do You Tell If You're Cruising?

One way of testing whether or not you are cruising is to examine the economics of your practice. Consider the formula in Figure 4.1, adapted from that shown in my previous Free Press book, *Managing the Professional Service Firm* (1993).

FIGURE 4.1

$$\frac{PROFIT}{YOU} = \frac{PROFIT}{FEES} \times \frac{FEES}{HOURS} \times \frac{HOURS}{PEOPLE} \times \frac{PEOPLE}{YOU}$$

$$= MARGIN \times RATE \times UTILIZATION \times LEVERAGE$$

The profit from your practice is found via the simple multiplication of four key submeasures: *margin, rate, utilization* (also referred to as chargeability or billability), and *leverage*. Two of these four factors are what I term Hygiene issues, while two others reflect changes in fundamental profit Health. The two Hygiene factors are *margin* and *utilization,* while the two Health factors are *rate* and *leverage*. To understand the difference between these categories, consider the various ways of improving your profit.

One possibility is by working more hours per person. Increasing your utilization means you made more money because you (and/or your people) worked harder. This is certainly an accomplishment, but it still is primarily a short-term achievement. To say you made more money by working more is not evidence of immense intellectual creativity. In fact, I call it the *donkey strategy*—achieving more by pulling a heavier load!

> **To say you made more money by working more is not evidence of immense intellectual creativity. In fact, I call it the *donkey strategy*.**

The point of any business is to find ways to make money *without* working harder. If I fail at making any other (real) improvements, I'll probably do that because I like the income, but I'll never puff my chest up with pride and say "Look at me—I'm a donkey: I made money by working more!"

However, if you can make more money not by working harder, but by getting the market to place a higher value on each hour that you work, then you will have accomplished something much more profound and long-lasting. By definition, you must have made yourself more valuable on the marketplace. If intelligent clients *willingly* pay more for your time (even when there are cheaper alternatives available to them), then you must have *improved*. Through some combination of ability, client service, specialization, innovation, or bringing in work that commanded a higher rate, you will have made yourself a better professional.

These two profit-improvement approaches (raising utilization or raising rate) may achieve the same (short-term) profit improvements, but their accomplishments are not commensurate.

The same argument can be made for the difference between margin and leverage. Improving margin is (mostly) about controlling overhead expenses—important, but nevertheless "hygiene." But if you can find a way to deliver your services to the same quality level with less of your time, using more of a less costly resource (technology or junior time), then you will have built an asset. To have leveraged successfully, you must have found new and efficient ways to deliver your services, to train and manage people to handle what they could not before, and to establish new methodologies. These improvements will not only improve your income today, but also serve you well in the future.

The summary is simple: By increasing either your rate or your leverage (or both), you're making strategic progress. You're being a Dynamo. If rate and leverage are staying constant, you're cruising. You may be making more money by working harder and/or by trimming your overhead costs, but you're still cruising! Working harder and cutting overhead costs are easier to do than achieving increases in your rate or leverage. No one said being a Dynamo was easy. It's just essential to your long-term success!

> **By increasing either your rate or your leverage (or both), you're making strategic progress. You're being a Dynamo. If rate and leverage are staying constant, you're cruising. You may be making more money by working harder and/or by trimming your overhead costs, but you're still cruising!**

Passion, Hard Work, and Success

The difference between Dynamos and Cruisers is rarely one of ability. Rather, it is one of attitude. The key to competitive advantage in professional services is not creative strategies, intellectual horsepower, or frontier technologies. (Most firms have these in abundance.) Rather, the dominant competitive advantage consists of *passion and persistence.* Those who win are not necessarily smarter than their competitors, but they do show more energy, excitement, enthusiasm, drive, and commitment.

One simple illustration may prove this point. The insight that says clients like us to show an interest in their business is an ancient one (I suspect that it is prebiblical!). Yet if you ask a room of senior professionals how often they read their clients' trade magazines, it is remarkable how few hands go up! They know they should do it; they just don't!

Any competitor who *has* made a regular practice of doing this should be able to engage readily in productive conversations about a client's business, well beyond the scope of the current assignment. At worst, this would be perceived as the professional's acting "as if" he or she *cared.* At best, the professional might spot opportunities to serve that client with additional work. The client, flattered and reassured by the professional's knowledge and interest in his or her business, might even *suggest* a new assignment.

What to do to win in professional life is easily (and broadly) understood. Show an interest in your clients, train your juniors, manage your projects properly, and invest in learning new things. These are easy concepts to understand. What seems to be hard for some people is finding the *discipline* to actually *do* them.

If discipline produces results, then how does one become disciplined? The secret is passion. If discipline produces results, then how does one become disciplined? The secret is *passion.* If you have to read the clients' magazines out of duty, you probably won't sustain the effort. If, however, you are *actually interested,* it will be less of a chore and more likely to become a regular (and not unpleasant) habit. You will then be likely to reap the rewards of your self-imposed discipline.

This reasoning extends of course to those who *manage* professional practices. If everyone in the group already knows basically what to do (and they usually do), the group leader's task is to get them to *want* to do it. In achieving this, the primary role and responsibility of a practice-group leader is to create excitement and enthusiasm. If this can be done, professionals on the team will accomplish more for both themselves and the group. More than anything else, a leader of professionals must help his or her colleagues to find the *fun* in being a Dynamo. Leaders must be *intolerant* of cruising, and demand (and help create) true achievement.

Unfortunately, dynamic leadership is rare. I have sat in on innumerable business meetings where the firm's leader

> **The primary role and responsibility of a practice-group leader is to create excitement and enthusiasm.**

presented a deep financial analysis "proving" how much more money the firm would make if everyone worked harder. Arithmetically correct, intellectually sound, and completely deadening to the spirit! Too many practice-group leaders are net destroyers of excitement, rather than net creators of it.

5

IT'S ABOUT TIME

There exists, even among the best professionals and professional firms, a perverse belief that *only* billable time (chargeable time spent serving clients) *really* counts. Anything nonbillable is viewed as either worthless or as not as valuable as "real" work.

While most firms have incredibly tight monitoring and control systems for billable time, few have effective procedures to manage their nonbillable time. This is a mistake that should be obvious to all concerned. What you do with your billable time determines your current income, but what you do with your nonbillable time determines your *future*.

What you do with your billable time determines your current income, but what you do with your nonbillable time determines your *future*.

Invested properly, your nonbillable time could help you to build client relationships, break into new markets, build new tools, train your people, or perform any of a host of other "asset-building" activities that determine your future success. To neglect nonbillable time is to neglect tomorrow.

How Much Time Is There?

Although it is unmanaged, most professionals already spend vast quantities of nonbillable time on their practice. Consider a typical accountant. In most countries, an audit or tax partner might perform (at a rough estimate) about 1,200 billable hours per year. Yet that same partner, when asked, will admit to working about 55 hours per week on his or her practice, for approximately 48 weeks per year. (Precise numbers vary by discipline and by country, of course: Cultural differences still exist in our homogenized world!)

This works out to a total of 2,640 hours per year spent at work, of which only 1,200 is billable but 1,440 is nonbillable. In other words, a *majority* of the typical accountant's work hours are nonbillable, unaccounted for, and almost certainly unmanaged!

The same would hold true for the typical consultant, actuary, PR counselor, and almost every other professional. It is also true of lawyers outside the United States. In American law firms, partner-level billable hours are often 1,600 to 1,700 per year (more in New York), leaving "only" 900 to 1,000 nonbillable hours—no longer a majority, but still a substantial proportion!

When viewed at the practice-group or firm level, the numbers can be seen to be quite staggering. A 10-partner practice group could easily represent a total of anywhere between 8,000 and 12,000 nonbillable hours being consumed per year. A 50-partner office might have 50,000 hours of nonbillable effort evaporating into the ether. It is amazing to think that very few firms have processes and procedures in place to ensure that they are realizing a decent return on this huge investment.

I often ask professionals "What percentage of your nonbillable time do you think is spent constructively?" The responses usually range from 10% to 35%, most of it dedicated to (unstructured) marketing activities. Professionals report that this time "just goes." They are working hard during this time; they just can't tell you at what!

I then ask a follow-up question: "How much of your nonbillable time is spent on activities that were planned and scheduled with a concrete purpose in mind?" Again the answers are usually well below

50%, and often close to 0%. Since the time is unplanned, it is not surprising that so little of it is spent constructively. When you don't plan your time, the urgent always drives out the important.

This is not just an institutional problem, but a personal, human one, too. The typical professional is working incredibly hard, often at a significant sacrifice to personal life. However, nearly half that effort is spent without producing concrete results.

The typical professional is working incredibly hard, often at a significant sacrifice to personal life. However, nearly half that effort is spent without producing concrete results.

There is a very real chance to improve the lot of the typical professional if he or she can learn to take charge of this vast quantity of unstructured, unproductive, nonbillable time and learn to put it to productive use. If professional life is to be more fulfilling and successful, and less burdensome tomorrow, then we must invest our nonbillable time wisely today.

New Time Categories

Professionals and professional firms should stop thinking about billable and nonbillable hours, and start thinking about three new categories: *income time* (serving clients), *investment time* (creating one's future), and *individual time* (everything else). The essence of this approach is to start treating investment time as seriously as income time. If your investment time is spent wisely on carefully chosen activities, you will have the ability to significantly affect your future success—and lifestyle.

Individuals and firms must develop the habit of treating investment commitments as equally sacred as billable targets. In reviewing one's performance in a given period, the test must not be *only* "Did I meet my billable targets?" but, equally seriously, "Did I finish the investment projects as I said I would?" Individuals and firms must learn that *both* are critical—that the one without the other is insufficient.

Alas, the rule in most firms today is that you are not only allowed, but positively *required,* to "blow off" any proposed investment time if it means additional billable hours. The concept of investment in the future is *not* taken seriously.

Notice that we are not talking about adding to the total number of hours worked. Rather, what is needed is the *discipline* of turning unstructured non-billable time *already being spent* into

> **Individuals and firms must develop the habit of treating investment commitments as equally sacred as billable targets.**

time filled with carefully selected actions that produce concrete investment results. Done well, there should not be, in the aggregate, any trade-off between reaching both current income goals (target billable hours) and (new) investment activities.

What proportion of one's nonbillable time should be treated as investment time and scheduled in advance? Clearly *not* all of it. Time is needed for "administrivia"—downtime between work tasks, reading the mail, collecting one's thoughts, and a myriad of other small activities that consume our daily lives. Furthermore, one cannot schedule all of one's nonbillable time and ignore the unforeseen events (proposal opportunities, personal emergencies, and unexpected client requests) that may place a claim on one's nonbillable time.

The sensible path is to start with a fraction (say one-half) of your available nonbillable time, and designate that to be spent on activities which will promote the success of your practice in the future. (Over time, the scheduled percentage may increase.)

For the typical professional discussed above (with about 1,400 nonbillable hours per year), this means approximately 700 hours for planned investment projects, and 700 hours left for individual time to deal with the usual nonbillable nonsense. This should be more than adequate.

Managing Investment Time

For those professionals practicing in firms, there is another question I pose: How much of your nonbillable time is contributed to a joint project or pooled with the nonbillable time of other professionals in order to create a critical mass large enough to seriously tackle a significant project? Again, the answers are depressingly low.

If there exists a practice group of say 10 partners, it surely makes more sense for each person to contribute his or her 700 investment hours (each retaining 700 personal nonbillable hours) to create a pool of 7,000 hours to invest in improving the practice, rather than having 10 independent decisions of 700 hours each. With a total pool of 7,000 hours, the team of 10 partners can collectively make sensible decisions on the highest return-on-investment actions to build their future, and can hold each other accountable for diligent execution of these joint plans.

Two refinements of this simple managerial process are worth commenting on. First, it is not necessary that an individual professional contribute all of his or her nonbillable time to just one group. It is perfectly satisfactory to allow a professional to choose up to two teams to belong to, as long as the rules of membership are clear.

To belong to a team means that you are *required* to contribute at least half of your investment time (i.e., 350 hours in my example) to the team's effort. Next, you are held jointly responsible with the other team members for delivering concrete results with the team's investment time.

Note that the teams that someone might join do not necessarily have to be from the department or practice group to which the individual belongs. For example, a tax practitioner may formally be in a tax department but agree to contribute to the investment effort in expanding the firm's practice in a given industry segment, or to improve the firm's overall recruiting effectiveness. A firm's formal structure for tracking its results for income-statement purposes does not need to determine the structure of the teams formed for investment purposes.

The second refinement of the process for managing investment time is to establish a three-month planning-and-review cycle rather than an annual one. In other words, instead of our 10-partner group deciding what to do with 7,000 hours over the next year, they should meet quarterly and decide what to do with 1,750 hours over the next quarter—and do that four times a year. This shorter cycle is more likely to ensure that the planned actions actually are performed. (For more detail, see the chapter "Fast-Track Strategy" in my book *Managing the Professional Service Firm.*)

Where Should the Time Go?

What are the best uses of your nonbillable time? One way of thinking about answering this is to examine Figure 5.1, where I list 12 business processes that every professional firm needs to do well. (Solo practitioners can omit items 9 through 12.) You may wish to evaluate yourself, your practice group, or your firm on how well you are currently performing these critical business processes, and prioritize those that you think are most critical to your future success.

The list is not presented in any particular order of importance, although it is only on item 1 ("Developing innovative approaches to solving client problems") that most firms tend to give themselves high marks. The other processes are done only modestly well, or poorly. For example, item 2 ("Finding new ways to lower the cost of performing professional tasks") consistently receives poor marks when professionals are asked to rate themselves. This is astounding, given that—in virtually every profession—fee pressure has been a fact of life for a decade or more.

Clearly, any group of professionals who could redesign their work processes to lower their costs would have a competitive advantage: They could pass the savings on to clients, take them as extra profits, reinvest them, or have any of a host of other options. Yet most firms are not working on ways to lower costs. Why not? Because it takes a well-thought-out program of investing non-

> Most firms are not working on ways to lower costs. Why not? Because it takes a well-thought-out program of investing nonbillable time to perform this activity—and most firms aren't organized to do such projects.

FIGURE 5.1

The Critical Business Processes of a Professional Firm

How well are you doing at the following numbered processes?

Which do you think are the most important to your future success?

Use the following scale:
5 = We're clearly superior.
4 = We're better than average.
3 = We're typical.
2 = We're a little behind on this.
1 = We're weak at this.

1. Developing innovative approaches to solving client problems
2. Finding new ways to lower the cost of performing professional tasks
3. Earning unprompted referrals from client work
4. Turning individual client assignments into long-term relationships
5. Continuously gathering market intelligence and tracking emerging client needs
6. Generating awareness of capabilities in important markets
7. Turning inquiries into assignments (sales-process effectiveness)
8. Developing new services
9. Attracting high-potential, compatible new recruits
10. Transferring skills to junior professionals
11. Developing and growing new partners from junior ranks
12. Disseminating and sharing skills and knowledge among partners

For which of these processes do you have an explicit investment program?

billable time to perform this activity—and most firms aren't organized to do such projects.

To make a similar point: Consider items 3 and 4 ("Earning unprompted referrals from client work" and "Turning individual client assignments into long-term relationships"). Both of these involve two factual questions. First: What percentage of assignments done for new clients turn into long-term relationships? Second: What percentage of your clients refer you, without being asked, to their friends and business acquaintances? Clearly, any professional who scored high marks on these processes would have a great future. Equally clear is the fact that it will take some investment of nonbillable time in client service and relationship-building to make these things happen.

The point is not that these are new ideas—they are not; they're as old as the hills. The question is: Do you have a structured, well-thought-out program for some portion of your nonbillable time to work on improving in these areas? Or do you, like most professionals, assume (and hope) that these things will happen as a result of the normal course of affairs? They won't. You have to work at it!

Next on my list are the remaining marketing (or business-development) processes: Gathering market intelligence, building awareness, winning assignments, and developing new services. These are usually not neglected topics, but firms vary significantly as to how well-structured and -managed their efforts in these areas are. Much nonbillable time is thrown at these issues, little of it in a well-planned way.

The final set of processes on my list has to do with creating the skill that professional firms sell: attracting recruits, transferring skill to them, and managing and mentoring them in a way that ensures that they will become valuable partner candidates; and sharing skill and knowledge among partners (e.g., having effective practice-group meetings that serve to make everyone a better practitioner).

Regrettably, but not surprisingly, this last group of critical business processes are among the least well-performed. The reason remains the same. It is not that no one believes in these things. Rather, individuals and groups lack the discipline to create structured programs to improve performance significantly.

I would not recommend that any individual or team should plan to work simultaneously on all 12 processes. The course of wisdom for any one planning period would be to pick out a small number of key topics, and design action plans to deliver real results in the targeted areas. Areas not tackled this quarter could be addressed later in the year. The trick is to get started and *do* something!

A Personal Example

Nothing we have discussed here is intellectually complex, or hard to do. There is much to be done, and there *is* (for most of us) enough time to do it. However, to *make* it happen, a revolution in our thinking is required. We must begin to really care about the future, and accept new disciplines in our work lives.

Let me give an example from my own practice as a consultant. Rightly or wrongly, I have decided that regularly writing articles is important to both my reputation and my future, even though I earn no income from them (they are not billable) and they do not produce any immediate sales. (Alas, rarely does someone pick up one of my articles and say "We've got to hire this guy—*now!*")

When budgeting my time, I set aside two specific days in my calendar for "Write Article." If a client or prospect calls and wants to hire me (at my full daily rate) for one of those designated days, I will do everything I can to get him or her to agree to an alternate date, since that specific day is *booked*. Saying "I'm sorry, that day is booked" is not that unusual—we're all forced to say it when we have another commitment. But how many of us are prepared to say it when the conflicting engagement is not another client, but rather our investment in our own future?

Naturally, I will be more accommodating and flexible to an *existing* client with a truly pressing need. However, a *new prospect* inquiry needs to be really strategically important for me to sacrifice my investment time.

> I will be more accommodating and flexible to an *existing* client with a truly pressing need. However, a *new prospect* inquiry needs to be really strategically important for me to sacrifice my investment time.

Here's the key point: Even if I have to give up that designated investment day to serve a client, that does not relieve me of my obligation to get the investment task done. I set (and keep to) absolute due dates for my scheduled investment activities. Even if it means staying up late, or pulling an all-nighter, I get those articles written. They are my future.

Each quarter, when my performance is reviewed with my coach (Kathy, my wife) we look at not only my income performance, but also my investment performance: Did I get my quota of articles written? No amount of extra income will buy me forgiveness if I fail to meet my investment targets, just as writing an extra article does not allow me to miss an income goal. *Both* are sacred. And, since Kathy is such a good coach, I make sure that I do every last thing I can to meet both my goals.

Again the point must be stressed: There is no *aggregate* trade-off between earning your income and making investments in your future. There *is* enough time for both. However, if it ever comes to a choice between my reputation and my income, I hope I'll be smart enough to choose to protect my reputation. If the choice is between my current income and my future earning power, I hope I'll have the good sense to go with future earning power. To act otherwise would be not only bad business practice, but self-destructive.

> There is no *aggregate* trade-off between earning your income and making investments in your future. There *is* enough time for both. If it ever comes to a choice between my reputation and my income, I hope I'll be smart enough to choose to protect my reputation.

6

ARE YOU WILLING
TO BE MANAGED?

I n a professional firm, you can manage only what the professionals will *let* you manage. To get anything whatsoever done, professionals must voluntarily approve and accept new accountabilities.
They must willingly vote (or at least consent) to give up their jealously
guarded autonomy. They must *agree* to be managed.

But why should we (autonomous) professionals agree to this?
Why would we accept limits to our freedom? Why must we willingly
accept additional accountabilities?

The answer to these questions is this: If people are not prepared to
be held accountable for what they do, it
is unlikely that they will achieve much.
Without accountability, most of us will
"cruise along" at a level far below our
real potential. The only issue to be debated here is what professionals are
prepared to be accountable *for*. They must decide which performance
areas, goals, and behavior are critical to success, and then agree that
they *will* be accountable for the execution of them.

> **If people are not prepared to be held accountable for what they do, it is unlikely that they will achieve much.**

A Conversation

I recently got a call from a partner in a professional firm who said that her firm had decided that its competitive strategy was to differentiate itself on the market through truly outstanding client service. As part of their program they had developed a client-feedback questionnaire which measured how well (in the clients' eyes) they had done on each assignment.

"Good idea!" I said. "What do you need *me* for?" "Well," she explained, "our service levels are good, but they're not improving. Our people *say* they believe in the strategy, and they *know* what to do—because we have developed some terrific training programs in this area—but they don't seem to be *participating* enthusiastically. We want you to come and give a motivational speech."

"I'm not sure that's what you need," I replied. "Tell me something first. When each client questionnaire is returned, does the managing partner or practice leader immediately examine it, and if it is not truly outstanding does he or she visit those involved, to discuss why a truly outstanding score was not received?"

"Oh, we wouldn't agree to that," she said. "We'd be worried that the client-feedback results would be used as a club to beat us up. We're autonomous partners with enough stress in our lives, and we wouldn't allow anyone to micromanage us."

"But it doesn't have to be punitive, does it?" I asked. "The manager's visit could be a supportive one, if he or she said something like 'Obviously the engagement went well, but since the client doesn't seem to think it was truly outstanding this time, maybe we can investigate why that is so.' Maybe the client is being unreasonable—but we *did* agree that truly outstanding was our strategy, so let's call the client and see what specifically he or she would like us to do differently next time. Why don't you call and let me know what happened? Or, if you like, we can do it together."

"I'm still dubious," she replied. "It all sounds very heavy-handed to me. Can't we just *inspire* people to do what everyone agreed to?" "Doubtful," I countered. Then I followed with "But tell me one last thing. If someone's billable hours were down, or bills hadn't been sent out, would the practice leader come to visit, to see what the problem was?" "Oh, sure," she said. "We've got tight controls on that. We *expect* to be managed on the financials."

I couldn't resist saying "Well, why don't you drop your tight financial controls and just *inspire* people to do the right thing in that area?" (I did immediately apologize for being a smart aleck.) She replied, "We've agreed to be held accountable for financial performance, but we haven't agreed to be held accountable for client satisfaction." "But you began this conversation by saying that you'd agreed to pursue a strategy of truly outstanding client service," I pointed out. "Yes, as a firm strategy" was her retort. "But we never agreed to be held individually accountable for it!" I had only one thing left to say: "Well, then you never really agreed to a strategy at all. To choose a goal without being prepared to be accountable for progress towards it is to choose nothing."

> To choose a goal without being prepared to be accountable for progress towards it is to choose nothing.

Autonomy Versus Achievement

Was this firm and its professionals foolish for not establishing the strict accountabilities I described, or better ones than I could devise? Not at all. It's every person's privilege to live the professional life as he or she sees fit. However, these people were foolish to think that they could achieve excellence (in *any* area) without being prepared to put in a forceful monitoring system to ensure diligent execution.

The point of this story is not to make a comment on client service strategies or the merits of feedback questionnaires. A similar story could have been reported in the area of people management, collaboration, marketing, or any of a whole host of other areas where individuals and firms routinely draw up wish lists or New Year's resolutions of things they intend to do—and then decline to design or accept an accountability system that will make it all happen. As the old saying goes, *intending* to do something is worth nothing: The road to hell is paved with good intentions.

There is little that professionals *have* to do in the sense of Immanuel Kant's categorical imperative. However, Kant also pointed out there is such a thing as a conditional imperative: If you want X, then you should do Y. No one told my clients that they *had* to choose truly outstanding service as a competitive strategy. But if my clients did, then there were certain things—like accepting personal account-ability—that they *had* to do to make success happen. If the clients were not prepared to do those things, then they shouldn't delude themselves by believing they could achieve their goals.

The best analogy I have found is one I have used before: that of a diet-and-exercise program. Like my client and their client service ideal, few of us need one more speech (logical *or* inspirational) on the wisdom and benefits of getting fit. Most of us understand and accept all the good things that will come to us if we live healthily. Similarly, most of us know what to do to get there. For some small percentage of the population, that's enough. Through simple self-discipline, these paragons get on with what they know they should do: They exercise regularly, watch their diets—and reap the benefits.

However, many of us (probably most of us) are not like that. With the best of intentions, we are still overweight nonexercisers. Believing in a goal, understanding its benefits, and knowing what to do to reach it all are insufficient to get us to change our ways. Self-discipline just doesn't work for us. And why doesn't it succeed? Because all improvements in one's personal *or* business life are just like the problem of losing weight and getting fit. First you must decide to make a permanent change in your lifestyle. Dabbling with exercise, or eating properly only a few days a week, simply will not work.

It is the same in business. You can't get the benefits of a reputation for truly outstanding client service—or anything else—if you treat it as an occasional thing to be done only when you can find the extra time. As many of us know, diets also have a structure that ensures first the discomfort and pain (the denied pleasures of food); the benefits accrue only in the future, and only if you stay on the diet. Human beings are not hard-wired to make decisions like "cost *now,* benefit *later.*"

> **Human beings are not hard-wired to make decisions like "cost *now,* benefit *later.*"**

Nagging Rights

What, then, will get us to change? For most of us, the answer lies in supplementing self-discipline with some form of external conscience. We must willingly, knowingly, voluntarily give someone else "nagging rights" to keep us honest regarding our chosen goals. For many of us, that someone else is our spouse. A few years ago my wife, Kathy, resolved to quit smoking, and gave me the right to nag her if she was ever tempted to weaken. There *were* times when I had to be her external conscience and (lovingly, but firmly) remind her of her objective. She reached her tough goal—she quit. By giving me nagging rights, she obtained bragging rights!

Notice a critical point: In marriages and in business alike, nagging is effective only when someone has given you prior permission to help him or her. Nagging about something that's one of *your* goals, and not one of the other person's, is amazingly annoying and remarkably ineffective.

Nagging is truly effective only when it is perceived as supportive, rather than negative or punitive. What does the trick is the willingness of the individual to accept accountability. In many ways, this is similar to an athlete's agreeing to be coached. A coach will exhort, demand, insist on one more practice, one more try. Yet the athlete *gives permission* to the coach to be demanding, because the goal is one the athlete has chosen. It's nothing more than saying "I believe in this goal. Keep me honest. Force me, if necessary, to do my best." Only in this way will superior accomplishment result. If you choose to pass on being nagged, or coached, or being held accountable, then you probably won't accomplish as much.

Another business example is given in my desire to publish articles regularly. I believe that, in the long run, they are good for my practice, and that I should keep to my resolve to write at least eight articles a year (it used to be more). However, like most other people, I find the discipline of writing (and rewriting and re-rewriting) to be a burdensome chore. I like the satisfactions of having written, but I definitely do not enjoy the writing itself. So how have I ensured that I will do what is best for me? I've made a binding promise to tough-minded magazine editors to write a regular column for their monthly periodicals. I've given nagging rights to outsiders, to force me to do what I should have the self-discipline to do anyway.

Democracy Versus Anarchy

Even if I've given a reason for individual professionals' agreeing to be managed, there still remains the problem of developing firmwide initiatives. There is a paradox at the heart of the term *professional firm*. The word "professional" has traditionally implied an extremely high degree of autonomy, while the word "firm" necessarily implies some form of collective action. How are these two concepts to be reconciled?

A professional firm's values, standards, and indeed strategy are not defined by what the firm says it aspires to, but by what it is prepared to enforce. A firm can get a reputation as a firm only if there are certain nonnegotiable minimum standards to which everyone within it must adhere. (For more on this point, see Chapter 8, "Values in Action.")

For example, a firm will never become known for its deep understanding of clients' businesses if individuals within it can decide whether or not they choose to meet this standard in individual circumstances. Firms must be *intolerant* on matters of values or strategy, if these are to be sustained.

> **Firms must be *intolerant* on matters of values or strategy, if these are to be sustained.**

The notion of being intolerant is not new for professional firms. There are two (and only two) things that are strictly enforced within the majority of firms. First: the rule that all their people will be technically competent. Transgress that rule and there will be consequences. One way or another, either through help, reassignment, or arranging for a departure, the situation will be dealt with. Technical competence is a nonnegotiable minimum. Second: the rule that you will not lose the firm too much money for too many quarters in a row. Break that rule and significant managerial attention will be brought to bear to tackle and resolve the issue. The firm (and the partners) will not tolerate a continuation of the situation.

And that's it! In most firms, technical competence and revenue production are the only two things you *have* to do. You may be *encouraged* to excel at many other things (client service, the training of juniors, participating in practice-group activities), but you don't *have* to do them. Doing poorly in these areas are not deal-breakers. They are not rules of membership in the club.

Why is it that firms have only two areas of intolerance? It is relatively easy to explain why those two are chosen: Firms usually enforce the things that will cause *immediate* pain if they are not done. If we don't send out our bills, it will cost us money *this year!* (Although, even then, individuals and firms often leave billing until the last possible moment, and then send out a disproportionate number of bills in the last month of the fiscal year.) What tend *not* to be enforced—and probably need the most external support, encouragement, and assistance—are the things that, if not done, will hurt us most in the long term. Those are the items whose enforcement is most needed. Yet building an overwhelming consensus to permit strict enforcement of these issues is hard to accomplish.

Part of the reason for this is the way that firm governance is structured. Many firms like to refer to themselves (with pride) as democratic institutions. The reality, however, is different—many firms are not democracies, but anarchies. The essence of a democracy is that issues are broadly debated, consultation is extensive, a majority position is identified, and (here's the defining moment) if a new policy receives majority support, it becomes law, and *everyone* must conform to it.

Many firms like to refer to themselves (with pride) as democratic institutions. The reality, however, is different— many firms are not democracies, but anarchies.

No matter how broad the prior consultation and debate, no matter how high the "supermajority" percent approval is set for something to become firm law, many firms have *no* ability to pass binding laws.

Rather, every partner there acts as if "There's no law that can be passed around here that I have to obey! I'm a partner!" Political science has no better definition of the term *anarchy*.

Again we must ask whether firms are being foolish in choosing this level of partner autonomy. Again the answer must be that people and firms are free to make whatever choices they prefer, as long as they acknowledge the trade-offs involved. If a firm cannot make a policy to which everyone must adhere, it will be literally impossible for the firm to develop a firmwide reputation, a brand image, or a common culture.

This leaves an interesting choice for every professional. Which kind of firm do you want to belong to? One that maximizes your autonomy (and, what is perhaps more significant, the autonomy of all your colleagues), or one that rigidly enforces high standards in various areas (beyond the basics)? This is not an idle, hypothetical choice, but one faced every day in a variety of professions.

In my career, I faced that choice at a crucial stage. I was teaching at a good, solid university that was very collegial and one that allowed a great deal of autonomy to every faculty member. At this institution, performance reviews of faculty were either gentle or nonexistent. There was very little you *had* to do to keep your job. As a result, most people were solidly competent, but not what you might call highly productive. Except for a few hyperactive self-starters, levels of accomplishment were modest.

Then I was invited to join the faculty at the Harvard Business School (HBS), where, as I knew, standards were very high, the pressure on faculty to excel was immense, and autonomy (while significant) existed within the boundaries of a palpably strong culture. My conundrum was whether to give up comfort, autonomy, and freedom from significant oversight in exchange for a demanding (albeit supportive) culture with high standards and enforced criteria for excellence. Because I wanted to find out how far I could go if I really tried, I chose to transfer to HBS.

Of course, one could argue that since HBS has significant prestige, the choice was trivial—it *is* worth giving up autonomy to join a prestigious organization, but *not* otherwise. However, the argument, I believe, is circular: It is the fact of high standards, rigidly enforced, that *creates* the accomplishments and the prestige.

Every professional, then, must make a choice about which kind of society he or she wants to belong to—one that maximizes autonomy for you and everyone else, or one that manages you (and everyone else) concerning certain key things. No one can manage you if you don't give them permission to do so. But, if you are interested in accomplishing as much as you are capable of, then I believe there are good reasons to grant that permission.

> No one can manage you if you don't give them permission to do so. But, if you are interested in accomplishing as much as you are capable of, then I believe there are good reasons to grant that permission.

I don't want to live in a dictatorship where someone can tell me what to do without consulting me. But I'm not sure I want to live in an anarchy, either. I want work in a democracy which functions according to high standards and shared values, both uncompromisingly applied.

As a professional, I think I and my colleagues alike should be held accountable for more than just financial results. As long as it is equally and fairly applied to everyone, I'll vote for a system with strict accountabilities in areas that I agree are important.

How about you?

7

WHY SHOULD I
FOLLOW YOU?

The first challenge in every professional's life is to learn *how to be* a professional. However, for many professionals, the time also comes when they must learn how to lead *other* professionals. This may come early, when the individual must learn how to lead a project team, or later, as he or she ascends to the role of practice-group head, office head, or one day, even a managing partner (or the like). Whatever the level achieved, certain key principles of leadership must always be observed.

Winning the power to lead professionals is no easy task. Before a leader can be accepted, let alone succeed, autonomous professionals must agree to be influenced by that person. Most professionals don't want to be either led *or* managed, and are highly resistant to *anyone's* making suggestions about how they practice, or commenting on their performance. Consequently, those

> **Winning the power to lead professionals is no easy task. Before a leader can be accepted, let alone succeed, autonomous professionals must agree to be influenced by that person.**

65

who wish to lead professionals must meet stringent criteria before they can obtain effective influence.

To explore what kind of leadership *does* work, consider the kinds of questions that are rarely asked out loud, but are on every professional's mind whenever a new leader is appointed or elected: "Why should I follow you? Why should I listen to what you have to say?" If a leader is to provide answers to these questions, four tests must be met: *motives, values, competence,* and *style.*

Motives

The first test that you, as my potential leader, must pass is that of *motives.* I will accept your influence and direction only if you give me evidence that you are primarily committed to the success of the group or institution, rather than to your own self-aggrandizement. Your task as a leader is to *help others* to succeed, not to strive only for your own success. If I don't trust your motives, nothing else will matter—because my primary concern is your *integrity.*

How do you convince me of this? Obviously I will pay more attention to your actions than to your words. Do you have a track record of helping other people? Do you have a history of bringing others into your client relationships, and passing on responsibility to them? Before you were even considered as a potential leader, did you make a habit of helping other people to succeed by contributing time and ideas to their practice, even if there were no immediate benefits or credit accruing to you? Can you show me examples of when you chose to put the firm's (or practice group's) interests first, even when that involved a personal sacrifice?

I won't settle for promises that you will start to do this *if* you become the leader—leopards don't change their spots. I look for someone who has already done it! Leaders are notorious for appealing to the need for team play in order to make the firm or group succeed. Fine, but what's your track record of being a team player when you were just one of us? It's all very well to be a role model when you've got the leadership job, but how good a role model were you before?

In looking for further evidence of your motives and attitudes, I might also talk to the junior professionals who have worked with you on your client assignments. What did they think about your leadership, managerial, and supervisory abilities in heading up a project? Did you keep everyone informed about what was going on? Did you hold project-team meetings? Did you take the time to teach and coach? Were you both demanding and supportive in giving out significant responsibility, and helping people to accomplish more? If you don't have a track record of being a good manager or leader on your client work, why should I think you'll be different if you become the practice or firm leader?

Values

If I am comfortable with your motives, the very next thing I want to know is "What are your core *values?*" I will accept your influence, guidance, and direction if (and only if) I believe that you and I share similar goals. I want you to have a personal philosophy of practice that I can be inspired by and share. However, I don't want you to tell me that you will develop such a philosophy *once you hold* the leadership reins. And your commitment to a *recently developed* philosophy of practice will not be credible. I want someone who *already has* clear values, and acts on them. I want to be led, if at all, only by a person of principle—not by someone driven by expediency.

> I will accept your influence, guidance, and direction if (and only if) I believe that you and I share similar goals.

As always, I will look to your past behavior to judge your commitment to your espoused values. Did you ever incur a personal cost in order to stand by those values? For example, if you try to tell me that you are committed to the highest standards of quality and excellence, I will look at your history. Was there ever a time when you turned away work (or refused an invitation to propose) on the grounds that you, or your group, were already too busy, so couldn't do a quality job if it added that extra piece of demand? Many professional firm leaders act as if they believe it's a mistake to turn away *any* current cash, as long as an "adequate" job can be done. Whether this is good business practice or not, such behavior cannot be described as an inspiring commitment to excellence.

Don't preach what you haven't practiced. I'm not inspired by hypocrisy. I'll be turned on by someone who both believes and acts on the principle that if we know we can't do a superb job, we shouldn't take the work. To engage my energies, you need to find some way to demonstrate that you care more about long-term success than about cash today. Similarly, I want someone who is more concerned with getting better, not just getting bigger—I may follow a leader, but not someone building a personal empire.

> **If your job as a leader is to influence and motivate me and my colleagues, then you must infect us with your personal enthusiasm.**

If your job as a leader is to influence and motivate me and my colleagues, then you must infect us with your personal enthusiasm. And I *don't* mean an overriding enthusiasm for money. If I am to follow you and accept your influence, I expect you to be passionate about our work, be fascinated with clients and their problems, and care deeply about accomplishing something meaningful. If making money is your primary goal, you will be a bad leader. Perhaps a great financial officer, but a bad *leader.*

The very best firm or group leaders inspire professionals to extraordinary efforts, not by saying "Work hard and we'll get rich," but by providing *purpose* to our professional lives. If you want me to go the extra mile and strive for true excellence (and hence make us *all* rich), then help me to find the excitement, the challenge, the fulfillment in what it is you want me to do. What has a chance of getting my attention is an appeal that says "Work hard, and we *really* can be acclaimed the best—not just in our own minds, but also by clients and competitors. Really try, and we can make a profound difference to our clients. If we succeed at *that,* the money will follow!"

Competence

If (and only if) I both trust your motives and subscribe to your values, I will want to know next about your *competence.* If I am to listen to you, I not only expect but *require* that you have constructive new ideas on how to improve things. It is often said that a leader must have a vision, but that is a misleading observation. Having a vision is easy: "We should aim to be the best, the quality leader in our marketplace, acting as a collaborative team, providing a fulfilling, developing, mutually supportive environment for all of our people . . ."—the words are *always* the same! What is hard is creating innovative approaches to practice that will help us achieve these goals.

So, in deciding whether to accept you as my leader, I want to know about your track record in coming up with new ways of doing things. Have you ever previously suggested (or, better, implemented) new ways to improve productivity? New approaches to client service or marketing? New methodologies, templates, or tools? New ways to train and develop people? Where is the evidence of your creativity in running any aspect of the firm's business? I'll ask everyone who has worked with you: "If you were stuck and needed creative thinking, is this someone you would turn to for helpful suggestions?"

I also expect that, if you come into my office and try to give me a performance review (as managers and leaders have a habit of doing), you will have some truly constructive suggestions for me, as to how I could improve, and thereby be more successful. Telling me that I should do better, but not telling me precisely how to, isn't leadership—it's merely offensive. Be **Be substantively helpful to me, and I'll listen to you. Otherwise, stay out of my office!** substantively helpful to me, and I'll listen to you. Otherwise, stay out of my office!

Style

Finally, if all previous tests have been met, I'll be interested in your *style*. Good leaders must be effective coaches, helping both me and my colleagues to stretch and to fulfill goals. This involves giving me (or, preferably, helping me to choose) challenging goals to accomplish. To be effective, good coaches must excel at two opposing skills:

I will not accept your guidance and critique unless you are supportive and nurturing. On the other hand, you need to be continually demanding, nagging me to stretch for my next achievement. One of these skills without the other is ineffective. If you are only demanding and nagging, you are Attila the Hun, trying to be my boss—and I don't take kindly to bosses: I *will not* follow you. You can force me into compliance, but you won't engage my energies. On the other hand, if you are only supportive and nurturing, you are a wimp, and nothing will get done. What I need, and will accept, in a leader is a friendly skeptic, a loving critic, a challenging supporter—someone not afraid to give both positive and critical feedback, and is involved enough to know when either is due. Achieving this balance is a rare but necessary skill.

As Peter Friedes (the former leader of Hewitt Associates, an actuarial, compensation, and benefits firm) has pointed out to me, most of us tend to overrely on either the one or the other of the two cited skills. For example, some people have a bias toward being demanding, and if that doesn't work, they become even *more* demanding— it's the only way they know how to lead. And it usually proves ineffective. Others lean in the direction of the nurturing, encouraging, supportive side, and if good performance doesn't result, they become even *more* nurturing—which is equally ineffective. What works is learning to play against as well as with your natural style, in order to ensure the most effective balance.

One other style issue is important: consultation. In a large professional firm, it is not possible for everyone to be involved in every decision. In spite of this, everyone wants to feel that his or her voice is heard, and views are seen to be relevant in decision-making. In consequence, I want a leader who engages in extensive prior consultation on major issues. I don't expect that my view will always prevail, but I do want my views solicited in a timely fashion—early enough to have the chance to make a difference.

Too many professional firm leaders hear that concerns about communication exist within the firm and think this means that they should *tell me more* about what's going on. This is dead wrong. I don't want to be told more—I want to be *listened to* more! Take the time to solicit my views, and be organized enough to be able to identify the forthcoming issues. Saying "There wasn't enough time to consult" is only evidence of your inefficiency.

Summary

In brief: I don't want the head of my practice (or firm) to be a cold, calculating "businessperson." I want someone who is not afraid to *care*—about clients, about quality, about senior *and* junior professionals, *and* about administrative staff. Someone who'll take the job in order to help make a difference in people's lives, not because of the position, the title, or the power. I want someone of whom it will be said "This is a better, more exciting place to work in since this person took over. We now have someone who believes in things that *I* can believe in—and that's proven every day, because we both do things differently now." Give me someone like that, and I'll agree to be managed.

As the old slogan has it, "A leader doesn't build a business—a leader builds an *organization* that builds a business." Accordingly, the single most relevant criterion in selecting firm or practice-group leader is finding someone who has an interest in building a team—someone prepared to get his or her satisfaction from the accomplishments of others.

> "A leader doesn't build a business—a leader builds an *organization* that builds a business."

There is an ongoing debate over whether leaders are born or made. The good news is that if there exists a sincere desire to help others, then coaching, leadership, managing—whatever you want to call it—*is* a learnable skill. The difficult part is not helping leaders to learn the skills, it's finding people with the right *attitude*. To be accepted as a leader, questions of motives and values come before those of competence and style. And since even past actions speak louder than words, leadership candidates will be judged by the behavior they demonstrated *prior to* trying to attain the role. You can't start being a leader on the day you get the job!

Professional organizations that have the type of leadership described here do exist, but unfortunately aren't the norm. What worries me most is not that today's professional firm leaders often are imperfect in fulfilling the role, but rather that many of them aren't even aiming at it!

What worries me most is not that today's professional firm leaders often are imperfect in fulfilling the role, but rather that many of them aren't even aiming at it!

I frequently encounter firms in which the practice groups have no logical structure, and in effect (if not in fact) are historical accidents: The people in the practice-group leadership roles are not chosen for their interest in being coaches, leaders, or managers, but instead on some other basis, such as business-getting ability or professional eminence. Too, the compensation system contains no recognition of either leadership *or* managerial activities. All practice-group leaders are expected to carry as full a client workload as any other professional—and then to manage on top of that! Of course, this is an impossible task.

This situation is not inevitable. The standards of leadership described here represent nothing more than a call for professionalism when managing professionals. All that is required is to find a small number of individuals within the firm who can be credibly received by their colleagues as interested in helping others to grow, develop, fulfill themselves, and flourish. A firm with no such people is in a sad state, indeed!

Part Two

(MOSTLY)
ABOUT YOUR FIRM

8

VALUES IN ACTION

Most firms have *mission and vision statements,* all of which stress client service, teamwork, and the goal of being the best place to work. They are truly inspirational and, *if implemented,* would certainly lead to business success.

However, what many firms misunderstand is that their standards and values are *not* defined by their aspirations ("We aim to be excellent"), but by what they are prepared to *enforce.* Something cannot be called a value or a principle if you are allowed to transgress it. Your firm can be said to have values only to the extent that there are clear, *nonnegotiable, minimum standards of behavior* that the firm will tolerate. In particular, whether or not your values are operational (i.e., actually influencing what goes on in your firm) is crucially determined by whether or not there are *consequences for noncompliance.*

> What many firms misunderstand is that their standards and values are *not* defined by their aspirations but by what they are prepared to *enforce.*

Consider the following example. A certain professional firm, one with a strong teamwork culture, had a senior professional whose recent book had received much public attention. Because of this focus on his public profile, he was bringing in significant revenues for the firm—but also operating in a way that was countercultural to the firm's teamwork approach. Among other things, he was—in building his own internal empire—refusing to share his leads with other professionals. He was also beginning to build up a cadre of "his" juniors who were loyal to him, rather than involving other junior staff who, in the view of management, could have benefited from being exposed to the kinds of work he was bringing in.

Despite much discussion between management and the professional about the firm's policies of collaboration and sharing, his wayward behavior continued. Others in the firm, aware of his success, were beginning to ask themselves (and management) "Is *that* what I have to do now to succeed here? Can *I* (also) get away with ignoring the firm's traditional approach, as long as I bring in lots of business?" The level of collaboration and teamwork in the firm was markedly on the decline.

The firm faced a tough choice. It had to decide what was more important—the professional's book of business, or the firm's culture and values. It was increasingly clear that it could not have both. If management of this firm was seen to tolerate the adverse behavior of this one successful professional, they would lose all credibility in trying to nurture teamwork and collaboration elsewhere in the firm. A decision had to be made.

Did they *really* believe that the teamwork approach was the right strategy, or should they have been less idealistic and more pragmatic? Should they look the other way and gladly accept the revenue stream from this "rogue elephant"? After much contemplation, they chose to stick with their culture, and asked the professional to leave. As it turned out, the firm continued to flourish mightily—as did the professional, in his own new firm.

The point of this story is that there aren't many firms with the courage to do what this firm did, which was to incur a short-term income loss in order to bet on the long-run benefits of sustaining their

values. In most firms, an economically productive professional would rarely (if ever) be confronted about softer "values" issues. As a result, very few firms actually have real, opera-
ble values. They *say* they do, but few of the professionals really believe that they're serious.

> Few firms actually have real, operable values. They *say* they do, but few of the professionals really believe that they're serious.

Much more common is the following situation. At a meeting of managing partners, I was trying to make the economic case for *enforcing* the basics of good project supervision—making sure that all juniors on every assignment knew what was going on in the total transaction, knew thoroughly what they were supposed to be doing, got feedback when they handed in something, and so on. Everyone present agreed that if all professionals did this diligently, the firm would achieve higher quality, eliminate inefficiencies, have more motivated juniors, and (not inconsequentially) make more money. Yet most of the managing partners felt that their firm's performance in this area was only adequate, not excellent.

Despite the recognition of the financial benefits of achieving excellence in this area, these managing partners felt that they had no ability (or, in some cases, desire) to mandate standards in this area, and certainly no power to enforce them. Behavior in this area was a matter of individual professional discretion. As long as professionals stayed out of trouble in supervising those working on their transactions, *no* real excellence was demanded of them. The prevailing attitude when it came to supervising younger professionals seemed to be "Good enough is good enough." Thus the benefits that would flow from true excellence were never captured.

Note that, in this case, the issue is not one of professionals doing "bad" things. Most firms would tackle a professional who was atrocious at supervision, or who engaged in indecency or harassment. Rather, the issue is one of *tolerance*. In most firms, the operating principle is "As long as you aren't causing high-profile problems, you're left alone." What's missing is any credible management behavior that *proves* that the firm has *high* standards.

Also note that no one disagrees with values, or the benefits thereof—whether we are discussing excellence in the supervision of juniors, or truly outstanding client service. All agree that it would be beneficial to attain excellence. The fight is about whether or not the firm (or its management) has the power, the desire, the appetite, or the willingness to *police* the standard. Sadly, most firms don't! There are no consequences for noncompliance.

The fight is about whether or not the firm (or its management) has the power, the desire, the appetite, or the willingness to *police* the standard. Sadly, most firms don't!

A similar issue exists in the area of client service. I recently interviewed a number of corporate clients about what they thought about the client-feedback systems that many professional firms have adopted. Clients said, in sum: "If the firms were serious about improving quality, we were willing to participate. So we filled in the forms, and waited to see what would happen. And guess what happened. Nothing! We told the firms what could be improved, and they didn't change them. We always suspected that firms weren't really committed to quality. Now we have the proof!"

Why didn't the firms make changes? Because most firms score "OK" on these client-satisfaction surveys, and that's why they're still in business! But by settling for "OK" as an acceptable response, these firms are (whether implicitly or explicitly) operating on that familiar principle "Good enough is good enough." As long as the clients aren't positively *unhappy,* the firm doesn't *need* to change! It has proven immensely difficult to get firms to go beyond this mindset and genuinely strive for "You're terrific!"

Yet the business case for striving for "You're terrific!" is clear. Any firm which reliably elicited that response, from either junior staff or clients, would clearly benefit from more motivation, productivity, follow-on business, referrals, and so on. The key point here is that the relationship between the level of staff motivation or client service and the benefits is not linear. The benefits come only when you are reliably, consistently *superior.* If you get nothing but "You're OK" you'll get by—but you'll get none of the additional benefits.

The missing element in the system is *management*. For example, consider what happens in firms with client-feedback systems. When client feedback comes back, firm management is usually smart enough to follow up and deal with clear *problems* where they exist. But if a client gives the firm an "OK" score, the professional involved rarely hears from management. No one ever comes around to ask "How could we have done even better?" or to say "Let's go to the client and talk about what we would have to do to get an improved score." Professionals quickly learn that, in the eyes of management. "OK" is *acceptable*. Therefore, all too often management does *not* demonstrate by its actions the "true commitment to excellence" that it loudly preaches when it launches a client-feedback program.

What is clearly needed (and mostly missing) here is what Tom Peters called "a passion for excellence." What I keep on discovering is that while I meet many individual professionals with such a passion, I rarely meet professionals who believe that their firm, as an institution, is *built on* such principles. Professionals agree to strive for excellence—but they rarely agree to be held strictly accountable for it.

> While I meet many individual professionals with "a passion for excellence," I rarely meet professionals who believe that their firm, as an institution, is *built on* such principles.

The standards of principled behavior are, in my experience, currently higher in dealing with clients than in either supervising juniors, or colleagueship with other professionals. Professionals live up to their espoused values much better when dealing with clients than they do with junior professionals—or each other! Yet the Golden Rule ("Do unto others . . .") is as applicable, and as internally efficacious, as well. Some professionals I have met are exceedingly noble when it comes to dealing with clients, but treat junior professionals, staff, and sometimes other professionals like dirt. These are the ones I worry about most: Because of their effectiveness with clients, the firm tolerates the professionals' bad behavior in other areas—and their bad example causes a decay of internal ethics throughout the firm.

This decay is all the more regrettable because there is a wonderful paradox about professionalism: The noble path wins! The more you

The more you act selflessly and give clients honest advice, even when it may be counter to your own interests, the more trust you earn, and the more future business you get.

act selflessly and give clients honest advice, even when it may be counter to your own interests, the more trust you earn, and the more future business you get. When trying to sell, the more you focus on trying to help, rather than on tooting your own horn, the more likely you are to win the sale. The more you treat younger professionals and staff with respect, and invest the time to supervise them well, the more you are repaid with energy, loyalty, and (not coincidentally) superior quality and productivity. The more you do favors for your colleagues, the more likely they are to help and otherwise support you in your practice.

What is fascinating is that this simple point seems to need stressing. Doing the right professional thing is not a *moral* point, it's just *good business.* If this is true, why don't more people get it? I meet more professionals who are cynics (about client service, about supervising associates, about collaboration) than I meet those who truly act as if they believe that doing the right thing is beneficial.

The following insight was provided by Richard Bland while commenting in a discussion group on Counsel Connect (an on-line computer service for lawyers). He said:

> This discussion brought to mind one of my favorite pieces of Biblical advice: "Seek ye first the kingdom of God, and all these things will be added unto you." We have substituted "noble path" for "kingdom of God" in this discussion, but the basic truth remains unchanged. It takes an extraordinary amount of faith, religious or otherwise, to live according to a value that is at least one step removed from one's more immediate needs—to view making money not as a goal but as a byproduct of a more noble pursuit.

Which brings us back to the importance of the firm. It is hard to sustain the faith, and the commitment to excellence, that Richard described if one is the only person doing it. It is easier if you are part of a community of true believers, all committed to practicing the same values. In fact, one could argue that it is only by having a common purpose backed up with *rigidly enforced* shared values that a firm can define itself. Without such common purpose and values, a firm becomes nothing more than a convenience for practitioners wanting to share space, support services, and a name.

> Without such common purpose and values, a firm becomes nothing more than a convenience for practitioners wanting to share space, support services, and a name.

What does it mean to have "real values"? It means much more than articulating desired beliefs. A firm will have functioning values only to the extent that it has an effective *management* system that is intolerant about deviations from those values. Most firms have—implicitly or explicitly—a catechism or creed which says in effect that to be one of us, to be a member of this firm, there are certain ways of behaving to which you *must* subscribe, including and covering the usual categories of supervising people, dealing with clients, and exhibiting collaborative behavior.

However, what firms also need (but mostly do not have) is a method to *enforce* these rules of membership in the "family." Enforcement would require two things. First, management must have a method of identifying departures from excellence. (Again I must stress that only being aware of *problems* is insufficient.) This information can be obtained either through formal measures, such as client or junior professional feedback systems, or by means of active, hands-on "management by wandering around." The informal approach is less bureaucratic, but requires much more managerial time.

The second thing needed to enforce values is yet more management time devoted to closed-door counseling and coaching discussions with those straying from the firm's values. Professionals must know that if they fail to strive for excellence, and settle instead for "OK," they can expect to hear the managing partner say, in private, something like "Come on, old chap—bad show! Not the way we do things around here, don't you know?"

Note that this visit is not about compensation or performance appraisal. It's about what is and is not acceptable behavior in this "club." Unfortunately, in most firms today there are very few nonfinancial things that would cause the managing partner to drop by. The range of tolerated behaviors is very broad.

It is worth noting a paradox about values and the role of management: When a value system is entrenched and broadly shared among the firm's members, managers need do little to sustain it, because everyone knows and adheres to "the way we do things around here." They also know that deviations will elicit a response. Little management time is required to *sustain* an effective value system.

However, where the value system is weak or nonexistent, significant management time and effort are required to build agreement among the professionals that strict accountability systems should be introduced to keep everyone honest regarding company values. An obvious, if old, example is the use of mandatory client feedback. It is one thing for professionals to agree that client service is a firm value. It is a completely different thing for them to agree that (for example) client feedback should be solicited on all engagements, and the results used to influence a professional's performance evaluation!

The key point here is not whether client feedback is a good idea, but whether the professionals are willing to work within *any* system that holds them strictly accountable for nonfinancial values. They must decide whether they are prepared to accept a system designed to be less tolerant of departures from agreed-to behaviors. For many, this decision would effectively be a vote for living within a society even more demanding of them (but probably more inspiring) then ever.

Finally, I am pleased to report a fascinating result from my consulting work. When I have had the opportunity to use anonymous voting machines and have asked the assembled professionals if they would support "this place" (their firm) in becoming less tolerant concerning departures from agreed-upon values (including a detailed description of what this would mean for their daily lives), the overwhelming majority vote Yes. There seems to be a hunger for the firm to stand for something and to have enforced values. Yet many *managing* partners I meet tend to say "We can't afford to be less tolerant. We'd lose too many people."

Most professionals I meet seem to want to belong to a firm with real values—but few seem to think their firm will ever get to that point. The good news is that there is an increasing recognition that real professionalism is both desirable and (in the long run, at least) profitable. Perhaps what professional firm managers ought to consider is that their biggest *business* problem may be that they aren't *professional* enough.

> **Most professionals I meet seem to want to belong to a firm with real values—but few seem to think their firm will ever get to that point.**

If you think this is not true of *your* firm, send around an anonymous questionnaire asking everyone to score the firm's performance, on a 1-to-5 scale, as to how well the place is complying with the principles contained in your mission or vision statement. The results may surprise you!

9

THE VALUE OF INTOLERANCE

It is a fascinating paradox that many high-performing firms in a wide variety of professions make minimal use—if any—of individual performance results in sharing firm profits. Instead, they use pay schemes that give significant weight to firmwide or groupwide results.

How do firms such as these achieve both prestige and high profits without relying heavily on individual performance incentives? One insight into the issue is given by how *other* professional firms, which rely on pay-for-performance schemes, deal with performance problems.

In a firm which makes extensive use of individual performance-based rewards, it is often the case that the firm's reaction to a mediocre or average performer is to say "That's OK, you can stay—we'll just pay you less!" This is hardly a recipe for excellence!

The responsibility to improve is understood to rest with the individuals, and the reaction of the firm is to leave them alone and respond solely through compensation. In such cases, clear "losers" are dealt with, but mediocre performers often are tolerated by top performers who still get *their* reward.

However, in a firm which relies mostly on firmwide or group rewards, all the partners or owners share the consequences if an individual's (or small group's) performance is down. Accordingly, other professionals (and the firm) have a direct incentive to take steps to help that individual or group improve, either formally through practice-group leaders or informally through the efforts of fellow partners. Everyone has a direct, vested interest in helping others improve.

> **In a firm which relies mostly on firmwide or group rewards, everyone has a direct, vested interest in helping others improve.**

Furthermore, in a group-reward environment, if someone's performance *doesn't* improve, even with help, the firm has a greater incentive to help the low performer find an alternative place to work. In contrast to the performance-based reward firms, the best group-reward firms create an environment of true excellence: You either are a high-level performer and are in the system, or you're not and you're out.

In other words, firms with individual performance-based reward systems often end up tolerating wide varieties of performance, while those with more group-reward systems are usually less tolerant of performance problems.

It is the issue of *tolerance* that influences the success of the enterprise. What is truly important in creating the high-performance firm is not the reward system *per se,* but whether or not there is an effective and functioning performance-counseling system that addresses performance issues. A *tolerant* group-reward system would be (and has been) a sure recipe for disaster!

In principle, an effective performance-management system can exist under *any* type of compensation system. Group rewards are by no means *required;* although they do seem to force a discipline that many individual performance-based systems lack.

Many firms with performance-based reward systems are fooling only themselves. They think that because they match financial reward with individual performance, they are therefore good at tackling performance issues. But the opposite may be true: The more the firm relies on rewards to deal with performance problems, the less effective the performance counseling tends to be—because performance issues are treated as the responsibility of the individual, not the firm. In essence, individual performance-based reward systems represent, in many cases, a perfect excuse to abdicate responsibility for coaching, counseling, and assisting (i.e., an excuse not to manage).

This syndrome often reminds me of the old psychology experiment about how to teach a pigeon the new skill of walking through a maze and tapping a metal bar so that it can get fed. Technically speaking, there *is* a single best way to teach a pigeon this new skill. First, you draw a line close to where the pigeon is, and if it can cross that first line (representing a small-first-step accomplishment), you feed the pigeon, commend it, and draw the line a little farther away. Then you feed it if and when it crosses the second line, and once more raise the challenge. In this way, after 10 or 15 iterations of such hands-on, one-on-one coaching, the pigeon will have learned the new skill, and thereafter will be able to find its way through the maze on its own.

What you *don't do* to train a pigeon is to explain "Here's the final goal. If you can get there, we'll feed you!" That way, you end up with a lot of dead pigeons! Yet that's precisely what in effect most firms' reward systems do! (The moral here? To create a great firm, management must run a system which *causes* performance to improve, not one that simply rewards improved performance where it happens to manifest itself.)

In influencing performance, firms have two sets of tools available to them: *financial controls* and *social controls.* The former term refers to the traditional set of measures, reports, budgets, and rewards designed to influence partner (and junior professional) behavior. The latter term refers, *inter alia,* to the face-to-face influence of managing-partner and practice-group leader behavior in conducting (usually one-on-one) formal—and, more importantly, informal—discussions with professionals. It can also derive from the small-group peer pressure (or lack thereof) in practice-group meetings.

The temptation to rely on financial controls to guide the firm can be overwhelming. First, they are quantitative—hence seemingly objective. Second (and of greater importance), a financial control system can be used without the investment of much managerial time. ("Here's the scorecard: Go!") Third (and of the greatest import), since over the years many consultants have ardently preached that you get what you measure, it is tempting to conclude that changing what you measure (or how you reward it) will always do the job.

This reasoning, however, is wrong—or at most only half right. In the numerous reviews of compensation systems that I have conducted, the focus requested by my clients is most frequently on these questions: Do we have the right criteria? Are we rewarding the right things? Are we paying the right people? While all three are eminently sensible basic queries, they often are among the least important asked when it comes to affecting the success of the firm.

Much more important are questions like:

- How good is the performance-appraisal and counseling system that acts as input to the compensation decisions?
- Do the appraisals that feed the compensation decisions result in substantive, constructive feedback and guidance to the person being evaluated?
- Does he or she know why they received the evaluation they did, and what can be done about it?
- Have other professionals pitched in to help the underperformer achieve more?

Remarkably, the answers to these questions are often in the negative. It is no surprise, therefore, that—even with performance-based rewards—performance often fails to improve.

Even more important in affecting performance than end-of-year performance appraisals are midyear, informal counseling and guidance sessions. It is a truism of management that the worst possible way to give someone performance feedback (and have it accepted as a constructive critique) is to save it until the end of the year and give it all at once, just at the very moment when his or her acknowledging of the critique will in one way or another affect compensation.

As every supervisor in business has learned, doing it this way will result not in grateful acceptance of the critique, and a determination

If you really want to help someone improve, the time to give the feedback is as soon as you spot the need, giving your critique in small bites and with no financial implication.

to improve, but in defensiveness, resistance, and denial. If you really want to help someone improve, the time to give the feedback is as soon as you spot the need, giving your critique in small bites and with no financial implication. Under such circumstances, your advice has a far greater chance of being accepted and acted upon.

Regrettably, such feedback and performance counseling (i.e., social control) is remarkably rare in professional firms. Not only are there few practice-group leaders (feeling that it is more important to stay billable) taking the time that it requires, but—as noted above—there is in many firms the atmosphere that performance is the *individual's* responsibility, and no one else's. Further, many firms are too "nice" for their own good. In the false spirit of partnership, they neglect confronting moderate performance until it turns into a performance failure, thus precipitating a crisis.

Of course, waiting until this point usually means that most attractive options are gone. When managing partners speak about the trauma of having to fire experienced professionals, I wonder why they do not shoulder some of the responsibility for failing to tackle performance issues *prior* to the crisis.

In stressing the importance of social control through counseling, coaching, and feedback, I am not trying to describe a gentle, Pollyanna environment. Indeed, my point is quite the opposite. Successful group-reward firms are vigorous in employing social-control techniques for the simple reason that they are *less* tolerant than other firms in accepting wide ranges of performance. The hallmark of such firms is a shared level of intensity.

The importance of shared intensity is illustrated by my experience in working with a consulting firm aiming (they said) to be the "truly excellent and clearly leading firm." We spent months figuring out precisely how to get them there, and came up with a plan that all agreed would work. But then one professional, in front of the whole group, said "We are all saying we want to be the best, and we agree on how to become that, but are we really willing to accept that much change in how we practice?"

I called for a secret (anonymous) vote with the following scale: "Vote 5 if you really want to "go for the gold", and vote 1 if you just want to make whatever changes we have to make to avoid ruining what we've got. Or you can vote something in between."

The result? The vote was split between one group with 4s and 5s and another with 1s and 2s. In preparing their strategic plan, they had all acted *as if* they wanted to be truly the best—but when push came to shove, half of them didn't really want that much change in their lives. Was either group wrong to make their choice? Of course not. It's each individual's free choice as to what to do with one's professional life.

However, the firm now had a problem: How was it to proceed? One approach considered was to attempt to use the compensation system to accommodate these differing preferences. Those who wanted to go for the gold and succeeded would be compensated for their efforts, while the others (who wanted a different lifestyle) would accept the financial implications of this choice. We named this system the "tolerant" approach.

However, the more we explored this possibility, the less feasible it appeared. Even if the right compensation levels could be determined, how would firm decisions on investments be made when there were fundamentally different goals? How well would people of different intensity levels work together? Could anyone really apply two different performance standards?

The more we discussed this, the more it became apparent that to function effectively, the firm needed its professionals to share one single intensity level, be it high *or* low. There needed to be a shared social compact. The firm needed to agree on a set of values, goals, and performance standards, and then be *intolerant* about everyone working to fulfill only those goals and meet only those standards.

Neither side was wrong—not everybody has to aim to be world-famous, and not everyone has to make a lifestyle choice. But it is hard to achieve *anybody's* goals (income, prestige, or lifestyle) if you're in partnership with others who do not share *your* goals. It was *nobody's* fault. They were just in the wrong marriage!

This conclusion is the same as that reached by the successful group-reward firms. They screen carefully for those who share their ambitions, and they are intolerant of moderate performance. They work actively with, and help, anyone who falls short of those standards. Their social-control systems are vigorous, palpable, and effective. People at such firms work hard not because they'll get paid more, but because they live within a society that is intolerant of anything less than the best performance.

None of this should be taken to mean that firms cannot or should not reward people at different levels. As I have tried to stress, it is (surprisingly) not the dollars that count in influencing performance, but whether or not the social-control system is functioning. Alfie Kohn, writing in the *Harvard Business Review* (November/December 1993) about the lack of effectiveness of incentive-pay plans in industry, said it just right: "Pay people well and fairly, then do everything possible to help them forget about money."

10

A TIME FOR HEALING

In recent years, many professional firms have done some pretty tough short-term things—fired partners, put pressure on those who remain, cut expenses to the bone, and initiated a host of other actions designed to preserve profits.

While many of these actions have been sensible, if not long overdue, they have extracted a significant price—they have fundamentally transformed the internal climate of most firms. More than ever, partners are questioning what firms stand for, and what it means to be a partner. The old social contract is gone, and no one is quite sure of what has taken its place.

> The old social contract is gone, and no one is quite sure of what has taken its place.

The following quotes are taken from interviews with partners in a variety of professional firms:

- "Everyone's focused on their own particular practice, to make sure their own numbers look good. No one's helping anyone else."
- "There's the perception here that you can fall out of favor very

91

quickly. Everyone's insecure. It feels like if you have one bad year, you're out of here."
- "Management have been acting like comptrollers, not leaders."
- "We feel like we're all here on an independent-contractor basis."
- "We don't take risks anymore with new ventures, because we're afraid to spend money—everything must be profitable straight away."

What is truly worrying is that these quotes don't come from either firms or professionals in trouble, but from highly successful partners at some of the best-run firms. Many outstanding professionals feel alienated, devalued, disillusioned, and cynical. Perhaps the most telling such quote is this one: *"I know I'm doing well now, but I'm still worried. This has become a young man's game. What if I can't keep up the pace? How's the firm going to treat me when I'm 50 or 55?"*

In many firms, the professionals feel that the underlying philosophy of the practice has changed. Where the "old" model of firm management stressed that if you did the right thing for the institution the firm would look after you, many believe that the new philosophy seems to be "Eat what you kill—as long as you can still hunt." A feeling of "We're in it together for the long term" apparently has been replaced by an atmosphere of "What have you done for me lately?" Instead of recognizing a strong company identity, professionals now see the firm as a loose affiliation of Balkanized, independent practices. In many businesses there is a fight (open or hidden) for the soul of the firm— a search for a new guiding ethic. In the words I have heard repeatedly: "There is a strong need for some optimism around here."

The problem is not just one of morale or motivation, but one that strikes at the heart of the effective functioning of the firm. If firm management is perceived by its professionals as short-term-oriented, risk-averse, and focusing on individual performance, then the professionals will respond in kind. Some professionals, motivated by what they see as self-protection, are participating less in firm efforts and acting more as independent contractors or free agents. In recent discussions of planned efforts to market to key existing clients, I have heard many comments like this: *"The firm has clearly demonstrated that it has no particular loyalty to any individual professional. My only protection is to make sure that my clients are loyal to me, not the firm or any other professional in it. My client base is my only protection, and I'm not going to let any other professional near it."*

What's to Be Done?

There is a profound managerial challenge in all of this. How are firms to overcome the new cynicism and regain the commitment and loyalty of their professionals? If firms can no longer guarantee professionals lifelong tenure (and clearly they cannot), then how are they to prevent professionals from retreating into believing that "They'll only keep me as long as I can perform"?

The answer lies in a very simple principle: Firms must not only *require* professionals to succeed, but actively *help* them to succeed. A firm will be strong to the extent that professionals feel that, as individuals, they are more likely to be successful as part of this company rather than of any other.

Most professional firms are very good at demanding that people succeed, but are pathetically bad at *helping* them to do that. If the goal is to create a high-performing professional firm, you *don't* get it by saying "We'll reward you if, individually, you can figure out how to succeed." That might work for the already talented, but it is singularly ineffective for those on their way up. The essence of high firm morale (and, not coincidentally, outstanding firm success) lies in the ability to create a firm wherein professionals *help* each other to succeed.

For example, how well does your firm measure up on these questions?

- Do those who are good at business development help those who are not getting better at it?
- Is there any perceived reward in the firm for helping others?
- Does the firm hold intellectual-exchange meetings regularly, so that professionals learn from each other (even though it means lost billable hours to hold that meeting)?
- Does the firm have practice-group leaders who are significantly less billable than the other professionals in the group, so that they have the time to coach, influence work assignments, and persuade the strong to help out those still learning?
- Does the firm reward those who develop templates, tools, and methodologies that others can use in their practice?
- Are there *joint* marketing efforts whereby the firm refuses to acknowledge, assign, or accept allocations of business-generation credit to individual team members, but insists that success or failure is that of the group?
- Does the reward system minimize individual performance, and base most rewards on group success, by dealing with individual performance issues as a matter for guidance and counseling, and not as a matter for a financial rap on the knuckles?

If, in spite of all this team support, you still find that someone has to be terminated (and of course this *will* happen), then what you want is for the person leaving (and everyone else who's watching) to say "The firm really worked with me to try to help me meet the standards. They gave me the guidance, the coaching, the tools, and the training, and I have to admit this isn't the place for me. They even went out of their way to help me find a place and situation where I can shine and be proud." Done *that* way, you won't have morale problems in the wake of a departure.

> **One tactic above all others is most powerful in helping professionals to succeed: effectively functioning, small-scale practice groups.**

One tactic above all others is most powerful in helping professionals to succeed: effectively functioning, small-scale practice groups. If a professional is engaged in joint efforts with others in building a practice group, then he or she will benefit from the exchange of substantive professional ideas, creative assistance on client matters, collective self-development through sharing practice experiences, mutual development of practice tools, and the hard (financial) and soft (satisfaction) rewards of building a shared market reputation.

None of these consequences of joint practice-group activity are automatic. They all result from a particular approach to managing practice groups which emphasizes the creation of joint intellectual property. They require that the practice group be active in holding practice-group meetings in order to exchange the latest ideas and developments. They require that the practice group emphasize the development of shared methodologies, tools, training, and marketing approaches. The essence of this approach is to ensure that the value to clients of the practice group is not embedded solely in the individual talents of individual professionals, but also reflects the accumulated wisdom, experience, and knowledge of the whole group.

The crucial role of the practice group (rather than of the entire firm) in helping professionals to succeed is derived from the following reasoning: First, mutual learning and assistance is most likely to occur at the small-group level. Second, even if there are firmwide initiatives that will assist, it is better to start small and go for the early success. Third (and perhaps most important), what many firms are missing today is mutual trust and loyalty—and this is easier to breed in smaller groups.

A particular emphasis on helping professionals to succeed should be given to business development. This should be organized as a team activity, with a number of professionals jointly executing an integrated plan to develop a well-defined submarket. For example, one professional could focus on writing articles while another develops a seminar, while yet another attends the client-industry meeting. Not only will such an integrated package of marketing activities actually work better, but professionals will feel part of something. They will perceive that the firm is actively helping them to succeed at business development, and not just requiring them to do it.

Another area of opportunity is providing professionals with appropriate support. In the name of cost control, many firms have cut back severely on support staff of all types—marketing assistants, secretaries, and the like. In my view, this has been a serious mistake, since it has left many professionals with the feeling that the firm, rather than providing the resources necessary to succeed, is hindering effectiveness. The wise use of support staff can make a significant difference in helping professionals to succeed. For example, some firms have marketing-support staff who research and produce briefing booklets on the latest business developments by individual clients, thereby enabling individual professionals to visit existing clients and more easily talk about those clients' current business issues.

Also important in creating a firm that helps its professionals to succeed is the role of the practice-group leader. In today's disaffected environment, firms must ratchet up the level of individual attention. You can't manage emotions by the numbers, you can only do it face-to-face. In tough times there's a tendency for professional firm managers to edge away from the coach role and become more like policemen, administrators, and bosses, watching the numbers like a hawk. Obviously this has been necessary, but so is coaching: offering suggestions, being supportive, providing creative ideas, and/or helping people to think through their roles and the best use of their time. Managing partners and practice leaders should aim to be participants in small-group practice area planning meetings, acting as a valuable, creative resource available to answer questions and offer ideas about practice issues.

> You can't manage emotions by the numbers, you can only do it face-to-face.

In many ways, today's professional is depressed. Professional life has become even more demanding, and professionals are looking at a future which requires ever greater effort for ever more uncertain rewards. This is not a time for rah-rah speeches. Asking or telling a depressed person to work harder or do more isn't inspiring—or very effective. What he or she needs is substantive ideas and concrete suggestions about ways to do something different.

Practice leaders should take advantage of every chance to find both new tasks and new roles for people. The emphasis needs to be on visible, achievable things. New approaches are sorely needed when people are "down." The thought of working ever harder is truly depressing; but give a person a new task to perform which he or she has never done before, and they may have more energy and interest. The lesson from Pygmalion is relevant here: Treat people like winners and they'll turn out to be winners. Unfortunately, being micromanaged *doesn't* feel like you're being treated like a winner.

In many ways, today's professional is depressed. Professional life has become even more demanding, and professionals are looking at a future which requires ever greater effort for ever more uncertain rewards.

In many firms, all that the professionals see from firm management is a bunch of tactics which come across to them as scared, nervous, panicky, and downbeat (tighten controls, fire professionals, cut support costs). Such actions do not convey optimism, so they must be mixed with clear signals that the firm is also visibly investing in its future. To restore optimism and faith in the firm, professionals want to know just what management is going to do to turn the situation around. They need actions that come across as new, creative, a smart idea, a clever response to the situation. If people see the firm management acting in a positive and optimistic way, they'll be positive and optimistic, too.

All business decisions require that a finite amount of pain be incurred. You get one of two choices: A lot of pain for a few people in a short period of time, or a small amount of pain for a lot of people over a longer period of time. Obviously the former is the wiser course of action. Firms need to get their short-term cost cutting and partner reductions behind them quickly, so that they can honestly turn to those who remain and say "It's over. Let's move on, and work to make sure we all succeed—*together.*"

11

HOW FIRMS (SHOULD) ADD VALUE

When working with senior professionals, I sometimes get them to estimate (anonymously) what percentage of their current success they attribute to their own talents, and what percentage to the advantages conferred on them by practicing in the particular firm that they are with. The answers vary, of course, but the overwhelming majority of these people report that they think they would be equally successful at another firm.

Of course, the question is biased—it doesn't prove that there is no value in the firm, but only that the senior professionals think that way. However, this, in and of itself, may be a problem in a world of increasingly mobile professionals. It is tempting to attribute this increased mobility (as many do) to disputes about compensation. My own research suggests that something more profound is going on. Put simply, many senior professionals believe that whereas they work for their firm, their firm does not work for them.

Many senior professionals believe that whereas they work for their firm, their firm does not work for them.

There is a serious competitive issue

here, because a firm has *two* ways of delivering value to clients. Either the clients obtain just the accumulated wisdom and talents of the specific professionals who happen to be servicing their work, or the clients can obtain this *plus* all the relevant accumulated wisdom, experience, tools, and methodologies of the *rest* of the firm.

A firm that can supplement the skills of individual professionals by bringing to bear its collective experience regarding each individual client problem is going to be more valuable in the marketplace than otherwise. It therefore behooves every firm to ensure that there is value *in the firm itself.*

Ways for Firms to Be Valuable

What does it mean for a firm to have value above and beyond the talents of individual professionals? What can a firm do that will help a professional to be more successful than he or she would be at a halfway decent competitor? There are numerous possible answers, including the following:

- Provide professionals with the benefit of shared skills and experiences within the practice group.
- Back up the professional with investments in shared tools, methodologies, templates, research, etc.
- Facilitate access to the skills of others in different disciplines.
- Establish procedures to produce well-trained junior professionals.
- Achieve a high level of referrals, cross-selling, and access to clients of other professionals.
- Provide superior support staff and systems (including technology), to facilitate conduct of the practice.
- Instill a system of supportive, but challenging, coaching to bring out the best in each professional, senior and junior.
- Create an emotionally supportive "collegial" environment.
- Provide for diversification of personal risk—in good times and bad.
- Establish a powerful brand name that makes marketing easier.

These concepts aren't new. However, it might be interesting to poll your professionals as to how well they think your firm is delivering on these *potential* firm benefits. (Try using this scale: 1 = Not at all; 2 = A little; 3 = Better than average; 4 = Terrific!) It might also be worthwhile to ask everyone to rank-order this list, to reveal which of the possible firm benefits they seek most.

What Does It Take?

Given the will, it's not difficult to create the benefits listed. Take, for example, that of shared experience within the practice group. To make this happen requires effectively functioning practice groups that deliver on the potential for intellectual exchange. Few firms have anything formal in this area. Practice-group meetings (when they are held) are filled with discussions of marketing, reviews of economic results, and budgets. They rarely involve substantive discussions of such topics as "What have each of you learned lately that's of value to the rest of us?"

Organized approaches to learning, it seems, often are restricted to training junior professionals—there are few structured programs to facilitate senior professionals' learning from each other. It is, in fact, easy to organize once-a-month practice-group meetings to discuss substantive matters of common interest. Apart from the substantive exchange, there will be a not inconsequential side benefit: Such meetings will create a greater *sense of community* in the practice, and a heightened sense of being engaged in a joint enterprise.

A related topic is the development of shared tools, data banks, specialized memo libraries, methodologies, and a host of other possible practice aids. Any firm willing to invest in these could make it easier (and, not so coincidentally, more efficient) for individual senior professionals to practice and serve their clients by offering thorough up-to-date research, speedy response, and lower costs through the avoidance of reinventing the wheel. And, of course, these practice-support tools would represent the intellectual property of the firm, not any individual senior professional. This may read like an obvious comment (which it is), but it is remarkable how poorly some firms perform in this area. *Rapid* progress in it, however, is being made by those firms which have invested heavily in such computer-based groupware as Lotus Notes.

Similar comments can be made about various market-research efforts. One Big-6 accounting firm is successfully marketing its "worldwide best practices database," a research study of business procedures in a variety of industries, which can be used by any senior professional to share with clients ongoing trends in that client's industry. It is not hard to conceive of equivalent pieces of research in other professions that would allow individual professionals to respond to client requests by saying "Yes, we're already up-to-date on that issue, and have material ready to share with you." That, instead of "I can research that if you'll pay me."

Since senior professionals will be more successful if they have ready access to trained juniors, any firm which has a systematic approach to training will have an asset that senior professionals would find hard to duplicate elsewhere. As before, this tactic of helping senior professionals to succeed would have the extra benefit of being valuable to clients. Much ink has been spilled elsewhere about effective training. My sole purpose here is to point out that a well-organized system for this can be (and in many firms is) a valuable, firm-level asset.

Similarly, there is little beyond the obvious to say about well-run support systems, administration, and technology. Done well, these things can make a professional's life significantly easier, and measurably enhance his or her productivity, not to mention enhancing that person's ability to render good service to clients. If well-organized, these systems can be a form of real firm value that is (alas) very scarce today, considering the cost-control mentality bred by the recent recession years.

Obviously, professionals benefit if they have ready access, on behalf of their clients, to the expertise of others in disciplines outside their own. In principle, this capability should exist within any multidisciplinary firm, but there are wide variations in the degree to which the necessary cooperation is forthcoming. In many firms, requests for cooperation are routinely met with "Sure I'll help—if you'll tell me what account number I can bill this to."

The test of cooperation (from either the senior professional's or the client's perspective) is not whether it is forthcoming when there is billable work to do, but whether it is there to bounce ideas around, get a quick favor, and obtain informal assistance.

This is more easily accomplished in small firms than in large ones. People who know each other well and interact frequently are more willing to do favors for each other than otherwise. In larger firms, and especially those scattered over numerous locations, this informal interaction is harder to achieve, and more-formal devices (such as interest groups of professionals serving similar clients) are needed to facilitate cross-disciplinary fertilization.

Do brand names have value? Do professionals succeed more if they are with a firm that enjoys a good brand name? Obviously there is something valuable there, especially if the comparison is between being a member of a brand-name firm and being in a small practice, or going solo. But what about the value of a brand name when comparing like-size firms? Would a senior professional lose anything by leaving the largest firm in town and joining the second- or third-largest?

What is often misunderstood about the value of brands is that it has as much, if not more, to do with *consistency* as it does with high levels of performance. Campbell's soup has brand value not because it's the best soup in the world, but because there is less perceived risk in buying it rather than a no-name generic brand. Brands, therefore, have value because they represent a form of quality assurance to the buyer, who can *dependably rely* on certain aspects of performance.

> **Brands have value because they represent a form of quality assurance to the buyer, who can *dependably rely* on certain aspects of performance.**

So it is with professional firms. It is not enough if the buyer obtains great service by catching the right senior professional on a good day. Brand value is created if—and only if—certain standards of performance are obtained *every* time the buyer uses the firm. To a very real extent, therefore, a firm name (and hence a firm) will have value to the extent that it has procedures to enforce its quality standards.

What of cross-selling and referrals? Some of my clients believe that cross-selling and mutual referrals are the quintessential core of firm value. They think that you cannot be an institutional firm unless you have institutional clients (i.e., strong, ongoing, multidisciplinary client relationships). While it is hard to disagree with the fact that institutional clients are very valuable, I am inclined to believe that they are a *consequence* of having an institutional firm, rather than its cause. In essence, it is the cooperativeness and spirit of joint enterprise involved in effective cross-selling that create institutional clients—*not* the other way around.

> It is the cooperativeness and spirit of joint enterprise involved in effective cross-selling that create institutional clients—*not* the other way around.

This reasoning raises the more basic philosophical issue of what a firm is all about. A group of senior professionals become a firm to the extent that they actually help each other out, whether in the ways described so far or in the innumerable other small ways that assistance, cooperation, support, and mutual encouragement are needed.

One professional observed to me: "At a minimum, there has to be some cohesion on a personal level. People don't actually have to *like* each other [although that helps], but they do need to have something in common, whether that's love of money [the weakest link], a practice area [i.e., a boutique], an ethnic background, school ties, and so on. At bottom, there has to be a commitment to the institution which is felt by all, so that there is no second thought given to helping other professionals, regardless of level, and to doing tasks that don't necessarily show up in compensation."

I think this comment is right on the mark. Firms must be bound together by something more than a compensation system. The importance of having *something* shared is illustrated by a firm which asked me to moderate a retreat between its two warring factions. One faction was involved in a transactional, high-intensity, premium-fee type of practice which demanded significant dedication, including long workdays and frequent weekend work. The other faction had a more small-business, relationship type of practice where the pace and the rewards were lower. These two groups respectively labeled themselves the Sharks and the Flounders.

We struggled mightily at the retreat to establish firm policies which would accommodate both kinds of practice. All concerned hoped that differences between the groups could be resolved through compensation system adjustments. Of course they could not, and the firm eventually split up—which was probably the right outcome in this case.

Neither group was wrong in any real sense. One group wanted the excitement of a fast-paced practice and the rewards that flow from it, and the other was willing to forgo high rewards for a more normal lifestyle. *Either* group could be happy and get what they wanted in a firm of like-minded souls. *Neither* could live with the other. Differences in intensity could not be papered over with dollar differentials. At bottom, there was no reason for these groups to be in partnership with each other.

In the final analysis, therefore, a firm needs to define itself by some sense of common purpose, common approaches, and shared underlying values. Fortunately, there is much that can be done to create these things through practice groups, technology, support systems, and joint marketing. Get started on the systems, and the philosophy will follow.

12

SUCCESS THROUGH
SKILL-BUILDING

Since professional firms sell skill, talent, knowledge, and ability, it follows that any firm that can outperform its competition in building and creating skills will gain a significant competitive advantage.

> Any firm that can outperform its competition in building and creating skills will gain a significant competitive advantage.

The need to be good at creating new skills (not just exploiting existing skills through effective marketing) is often overlooked. Most firms recruit from the same talent pool as their major competitors, and all begin with similar raw material—the bright, entry-level professional. Each firm faces the task of transforming this raw material, through a process of work assignment, supervision, coaching, and training, into the finished product: the fully developed professional. Competitive advantage does not come from an ability to hire better people than your competitors do, but from a superior ability to develop them.

Few firms emphasize the rapid creation of new skills. For example, even though most firms fervently preach the importance of good

105

coaching of their juniors, those juniors will tell you that little more than lip service is given to this in the daily operations of the practice. Helping junior professionals to learn thoroughly and quickly is low on partners' daily priority lists, and thus rarely commands their prime attention. As a result, most learning is opportunistic, disorganized, haphazard, and slow—in fact, usually the responsibility of the junior professional himself or herself. (Here we have the infamous "sink or swim" system prevalent at so many firms.)

The Benefits of Skill-Building

I frequently ask firms "What advantages would you get if you outperformed your competitors at skill-building at all levels?" Among the answers they list are:

- Higher-quality work product
- Increased ability to delegate with confidence, and hence less stress on senior professionals
- Fewer write-offs of unproductive time spent by junior professionals
- Greater junior professional morale and enthusiasm, leading to better productivity and efficiency
- Lower turnover of junior professionals, and hence lower recruiting costs
- A higher caliber of recruits, due to a spreading reputation for excellent training
- Greater client acceptance of using junior professionals on engagements (and hence higher leverage), if they are seen to be well trained
- Over time, earn (and deserve) higher fees, due to higher skill levels

If these benefits are real, why is it that skill-building is so often neglected? My observations suggest that this lack of attention is explained by a number of myths about training and skill-building that are commonly held among professional service firms. Let's examine a few of them.

Myth One: Training Is Expensive

As the bumper sticker reads, "If you think education's expensive, try ignorance." So it is with training—if you think it's expensive, try having untrained people. Of course, training should not be viewed as a cost, but as an investment. The issue is not whether the expenditure is high, but how certain are the returns on this investment.

> So it is with training—if you think it's expensive, try having untrained people.

Although it's hard to find scientific proof of the value of training, it is nevertheless instructive to look at some firms reputed to have a strategy of heavy investments in training. Among these are McKinsey (strategy consultants) and Arthur Andersen (accountants.) These firms have reputations both for the highest per-capita training invest-ments as well as for being among the most profitable firms in their re-spective professions.

Arthur Andersen claims to spend the equivalent of 7% of its rev-enues on training. If one assumes a 2,000-hour year, this translates into 140 hours, or approximately 14 days, of training for every pro-fessional in the firm, including partners. The point here is that there are at least a few firms which have demonstrated that high training expenditures are not incompatible with extremely high profits per partner.

Myth Two: Skill-Building Is for the Junior Professionals

It should be obvious that, to excel at skill-building, a firm should not only require *every* professional within it to continuously learn and grow, but also that it needs to be superior in helping them to do so. On top of that, all its systems, rewards, encouragements, perfor-mance counselings, and so on that are necessary for this to succeed must function well.

To begin with, all professionals should be expected to have a per-sonal career strategy for making themselves continually more valu-able in the marketplace. They should constantly be searching for new areas of practice to get involved in, and should eagerly be seeking ways to delegate the more familiar parts of their client work. There should be little or no tolerance for cruising.

Professionals should be assessed less on the sheer volume of work that they do, and more on the *type* of work they do, and its quality.

Professionals should be assessed less on the sheer volume of work that they do, and more on the *type* of work they do, and its quality. To make all of this happen, a thorough reexamination of the professional performance-counseling and compensation system is needed to ensure that the correct incentives are in place.

There should be no tolerance for underdelegation. If a portion of a professional's work can be done with quality by a more junior person under proper supervision, there should be a requirement for that professional to ensure that the work is always assigned to the lowest level capable of producing quality work under supervision. In this way, the senior professional would be free to pursue and take on more-challenging, asset-building activities. Again, a thorough reexamination of the measure-and-reward system would be needed to ensure that the firm's systems encourage and reward effective delegation. Few such systems do that today.

To ensure that the firm continues to provide fast skill-building opportunities to partners and nonpartners alike, the company must manage its practice-development activities very carefully. It is hard to be a fast skill-building firm if a high percentage of the work is repetitive and routine. One of the essential ingredients in executing the fast skill-building strategy is an active pursuit of frontier, asset-building work. Accordingly, the firm would need a well-organized, constant push to upgrade the caliber of work brought in, and must be disciplined in avoiding the trap of pursuing too much work for volume reasons alone.

Myth Three: Skill-Building Should Be the Responsibility of a Training Director

The word *training* tends to evoke formal, classroom-setting programs—but such are not its only meaning. Most people would readily agree that the need is not just for training, but also for skill-building. Similarly, most people would further agree that the overwhelming majority of skill-building in professional life takes place *on the job*.

One of the essential ingredients in executing the fast skill-building strategy is an active pursuit of frontier, asset-building work.

However, this does not happen automatically. Whether skill-building on the engagement is fast or slow depends upon how the lead professional running the engagement manages it. In a firm that really cared about skill-building, *all* professionals would be required to function as effective coaches, by taking their engagement-supervision duties seriously. Everyone on the engagement would be involved in team strategy sessions, allowing all concerned to learn by observing, as well as by participating in the thought process that leads to decisions made on how to handle the engagement.

Lead professionals would be thoughtful about giving stretching (but well-supervised) tasks to individuals as soon as they were ready for them. They would be effective in ensuring that those to whom the work is assigned understand precisely what is expected in terms of output, scope, format, budget, and due dates. Every person on the engagement would understand where his or her piece fit into the overall strategy for the case or deal.

Lead professionals would take the time at the point of initial work assignment to offer advice on the best way to approach the work, what resources are available, and so on. Monitoring meetings and checkpoints would be scheduled to ensure that the work is on track, and to offer midcourse guidance. Prompt, constructive feedback would be given on each piece of work, and supervising professionals would use errors as an opportunity to teach, not punish. (Note that what we have described here is not a mentoring system; *that* term usually refers to some off-the-engagement guidance-counselor system which has been tested and failed.)

Few, if any, of these on-the-engagement supervisory behaviors take great skill or talent to perform. What is required is the willingness to devote the time and discipline to do it—*every* time. Of course, none of this is news. Most professionals would report that the most important part of their own development was the opportunity to work with a senior professional and carefully observe him or her in action.

Many people point out that clients used to pay for these activities to take place, but are no longer willing to do so. The absence of such funding is not an excuse to forgo training, though many firms are reacting as if it were. Training is a cost of doing business, and the fact that clients won't pay for it anymore should evoke the reaction "Welcome to the real world, folks!"

> **Training is a cost of doing business, and the fact that clients won't pay for it anymore should evoke the reaction "Welcome to the real world, folks!"**

Myth Four: It's Not Worth Training Those Who'll Leave

One of the most commonly offered rationalizations of why firms underinvest in training is the "up-or-out" culture. The argument often proffered is that "Many of the junior professionals are going to leave, so why train them?" A variation on this that I hear frequently is "If we train them, they'll either want my job or will be so qualified that they'll leave." Of course, there is circular reasoning here. The less a firm cares about junior professional development, the more likely the juniors *are* to leave, and it's always the best who are the most mobile. The weak, untrained ones will stay as long as they can.

The up-or-out system is not a justification to underinvest in training. What McKinsey and Arthur Andersen (as well as other elite firms wherein it is difficult to make partner) say to their juniors is (in effect): "While only a small percentage of you will ever make partner, we're going to make sure that your time with us is as developmental as you can conceive of getting in this profession. And you'll leave with great career opportunities, and be a loyal alumnus/a who is a lifelong friend of the firm."

The result of this approach appears to be high levels of productivity, efficiency, quality, and responsiveness. If part of the cost of getting those things is training everyone (not just those who will stay), then it would appear to be money and time well spent.

Myth Five: Training Doesn't Work (We Tried It and Failed)

Having argued that many firms underinvest in training (or skill-building), let me now argue that many firms waste a significant portion of their training budget.

I have frequently been asked to conduct a training program on a "new" skill as a means of changing attitudes or behavior in the practice. The training programs usually go well enough, but frequently the participants return to their practice feeling subject to the same pressures, measurements, and rewards as before—and there is little change in behavior. These experiences have taught me that training is a great last step but a pathetic first step. It is sensible to make training available when the professionals are already convinced that they need to learn a new skill, but you can't change people by first putting on a training program.

I admire those firms that do not rely too heavily on outsiders to conduct their training. The best firms, in my view, share a philosophy of having most of their training conducted by their own professionals— often senior partners. In consequence, the training is real, practical, and believable (which outsiders often aren't), and has a meaningful impact.

> The best firms, in my view, share a philosophy of having most of their training conducted by their own professionals—often senior partners.

Too many firms rely on outside consultants to do their training, reasoning that their own senior professionals are better off keeping busy serving clients. Needless to say, this is a very short-term view, and a misguided one. As one practitioner pointed out to me, there is another benefit when insiders do the training— senior professionals *also* learn when they teach their specialty to younger professionals. Of course, not all insiders are good at teaching, and that is precisely the point: They should be! There is a need to use outsiders to train the trainers, but firms should wean themselves off of outside trainers if they want to reap the real benefits of training.

Myth Six: Skill-Building Should Focus Primarily on Technical Matters

Most firms are pretty good at training their people in the technical core of their profession, but few work actively at developing some of the critical skills that determine the professional's success. There is, of course, a difference between (for example) being knowledgeable in the law and being skilled at lawyering (or being a consultant and knowing how to be a counselor). Much of the latter has traditionally been learned by osmosis, but is indeed trainable.

It is possible, for example, to help people to learn how to work with clients, how to explain things to them, how to see things from their point of view, and how to bring them bad news in such a way that they thank you rather than shoot the messenger. These counseling skills are not the same as selling skills (which some firms do teach). Materials in this area exist, but few firms make extensive use of them as training aids.

Additional training or skill areas can be identified. Since most professionals serve business corporations, there is a real opportunity to make the firm's professionals more valuable by helping them to develop the skills of understanding business issues, or of diagnosing and discussing business problems. For example, a lawyer who understands only the law and knows nothing about business will be limited in his or her ability to understand and work with clients. The same, of course, is true of accountants, actuaries, and even management consultants who know their own fields but sometimes have a limited understanding of either general business issues or the specific problems of a client industry.

> **A lawyer who understands only the law and knows nothing about business will be limited in his or her ability to understand and work with clients.**

Myth Seven: We Can Change Training
Without Changing How We Manage

To excel at skill-building, firms need to find a way to get *every* lead professional to live up to his or her responsibility to coach on each engagement. Can this be done? Yes, but only under one condition: that there is an effective performance-appraisal system which rewards those who do it, and penalizes those who do not. There must be *consequences* for noncompliance.

Such systems do exist. One mild version is to have practice-group leaders poll the junior professionals (anonymously if necessary) to learn which among them are terrific at this, and which are not. That data should be a formal part of all professionals' performance evaluation. Firm management has to have the courage to tackle professionals who are weak in this performance area.

Finding out who's good at this and who's not is not the difficult part. The hard part is getting firm management and compensation committees to deal with the underperformers. The basic attitude in most firms is that if you're good or OK at business generation, personal billings, and so on, then your performance on coaching is sort of irrelevant. As always, the issues are those of values and their enforcement.

One training partner noted the following: "The kicker [in this operation] will be tying training to the evaluation system. Our Committee on Training recognized the need to link training and evaluations several years ago, but the task of implementing a program based on this premise has been thwarted repeatedly by the realities of the billable-hour system. We do what we can to cajole, demand, and beg attendance at our programs, and often succeed at filling chairs. Unfortunately, that success has often been at the expense of some poor junior who dutifully sits through a training session completely distracted by fear and anxiety over this 'waste' of precious time."

This is the same old issue—firm value systems, reflected in management systems, that have embedded in their core

> The same old issue—firm value systems, reflected in management systems, that have embedded in their core an unwillingness to invest in the future.

an unwillingness to invest in the future. Most firms' knee-jerk reaction to every training hour or dollar is that it represents yet one more lost degree of utilization and reduction in this year's profit. Thus "investment" is, in this case, just a dirty word. And until this attitude changes, there's no hope.

13

WHAT KIND OF PROVIDER ARE YOU?

One of the most common sources of problems in professional life comes when professionals employ managerial processes that may be well suited to one type of professional practice, but completely inappropriate for another. How a practice should be run depends critically upon how it is *positioned* (i.e., which key benefit the client wants to buy).

Some differences between types of practice are shown in Figure 13.1, which gives a method of categorizing professional practices, using two key dimensions: First, the degree of customization necessary to solve the client's problem; and second, the degree of client contact that the client requires in the delivery of the service. These dimensions define four kinds of professional practice which we will respectively refer to as Pharmacist, Nurse, Brain Surgeon, and Psychotherapist.

The Pharmacist

A Pharmacist (or Chemist, as it would be called in Commonwealth countries) practice is one in which the client is trying to buy a rela-

FIGURE 13.1

	Standardized Process Emphasis on Execution	Customized Process Emphasis on Diagnosis
High degree of client contact. Value is rendered in the "front room," i.e., during interraction with the client.	NURSE	PSYCHOTHERAPIST
Low degree of client contact. Value is rendered in the professional's "back room." Client focus is on result only.	PHARMACIST	BRAIN SURGEON

tively familiar service and does not require very much counseling, consultation, or contact.

The client wants the service performed to strict technical standards at a minimal cost. This type of practice is defined as a standardized *process* which is conducted with little, if any, client contact. This does not mean that the *result* cannot be highly customized, but merely that the process to be followed in producing the result is well specified.

Quality standards, in the sense of "conformance to specifications" must be high, since the client will be swallowing the pills. However, the client does not require that the pill be specifically designed for him or her. The client wants to buy well-established methodologies and procedures, not innovation and creativity.

The client is, in effect, saying "I have a headache, and I know that you, along with many others, are licensed to make aspirin. Don't waste your time and mine trying to convince me that it's brain surgery that I need. I've done this before, and I can tell for myself the difference between the needs for aspirin and brain surgery. I want aspirin! What's your best price?"

The Nurse

The Nursing practice also delivers relatively familiar, or "mature," services that do not require high levels of innovation. However, it differs from the Pharmacist practice in that the emphasis is not only on the ability to make the pill (which still may be required), but also on the ability to counsel and guide the client through the process. This time, the client wants to be nurtured and nursed: "Help me to understand what's going on; explain to me what you're doing and why; involve me in the decision-making; help me to understand my options. Be with me and interact with me throughout the process, until this is all over. I need a front-room advisor, not a back-room technician."

The Brain Surgeon

The Brain Surgeon combines high levels of customization, creativity, and innovation with a low degree of client interaction. The client is searching for a practitioner who is at the leading edge of his or her discipline, and who can bring innovative thinking to bear on a unique assignment. Here, the client says: "I have a bet-your-company problem. Save me! I don't want to know the details; just find the right answer! If I wake up in the morning, I'll pay your outrageous bill! I'm not shopping on price, I'm trying to find the most creative provider I can."

The Psychotherapist

Finally, the Psychotherapist practice is one wherein the client says: "Again I have a bet-your-company problem, only this time I don't want you to give me the anesthetic and leave me out of the process. I want to be intimately involved in the problem-solving process. What I'm really trying to buy is someone who can sit down with me and help me to understand why my company is falling apart, how I differentiate between a symptom and a cause, and what I *must* deal with and what I can afford to postpone. Sit down with me and my executive team, and help us to understand our problem and our options."

As with the Brain Surgeon, the emphasis in being a Psychotherapist is as much about diagnosis as it is about execution. When buying the services of a Nurse or Pharmacist, clients know what they want done; they are hiring someone to execute it. But with Brain Surgeons and Psychotherapists, the clients are seeking help on what needs to be done, as well as on how to do it.

Differences Between Practices

There is a market for all four of these kinds of providers, and they all represent honorable ways of being of value to clients. However, the key message in Figure 13.1 is that the four services described represent a quartet of profoundly different businesses. Virtually everything—from marketing to hiring, from managerial styles to economics, from key skills to performance-appraisal criteria—varies significantly, depending on which service you are trying to provide.

Consider, for example, how each of these providers makes money. The Pharmacist is in a fee-sensitive business, where the key to economic success lies in finding ways to "make the aspirin" at a very low cost, without compromising quality. This means getting the work done with a minimum of high-priced senior professional time, and extensive use of either low-cost (junior) time or such time-saving tools as methodologies, systems, templates, and procedures. The Pharmacist is in a low-fee, high-leverage business.

The Nurse also needs to have well-established procedures, methodologies, and tools, but if the Nurse has superior counseling skills, then he or she can command higher fees than the aspirin maker. Since the client is buying a relationship with the primary-care provider, clients will be less inclined to shop on price, and more likely to pay a premium for an advisor they can work well with and trust.

However, since much of the work is likely to involve client contact, there is probably a little less chance to leverage (by using low-priced junior professionals) for the front-room portion of the work. The Nurse thus makes money by charging higher fees than the aspirin-maker, but probably employs lower leverage.

The Brain Surgeon is paid for innovation, creativity, and frontier technical skills. Accordingly, the Brain Surgeon has even less ability to get projects done by leveraging junior resources or established methodologies. Instead, the Brain Surgeon makes money if (and only if) he or she is truly recognized by the market as being a leading practitioner who can charge premium fees. Brain surgeons make money through high fees and low-to-modest leverage.

(In fact, the fees you can charge are a pretty good test of whether or not you *are* a Brain Surgeon. If you can charge more than your competition, you are. If you have to win your business by giving discounts or entering into price competition, then admit that the market *does not* view you as special. You're not a Brain Surgeon? Get into the aspirin factory!)

The Psychotherapist has the most unleveraged business of all. Since most of the work is face-to-face counseling at the highest level of the client organization, little use can be made of junior staff (except for background analytical work in support of the Psychotherapist's efforts).

The Psychotherapist makes money in one of two ways: Either high fees are charged, or work results from his or her diagnosis that can be referred to other parts of the "hospital." In other words, the Psychotherapist may not be very profitable on a stand-alone basis, but makes money by being a "relationships manager" and generating work for others.

All of this is summarized in Figure 13.2, which shows the key skills required of each practitioner, and the respective key economic drivers.

FIGURE 13.2

	Standardized Process (Execution)	Customized Process (Diagnosis)
High degree of client contact.	**Nurse** **Key Skill:** Making Client Experience Comfortable and User-Friendly in Going Through Pre-Set Process **Profit Drivers:** Above-Average Fees. Good Leverage, Established Procedures	**Psychotherapist** **Key Skill:** Real-Time Diagnosis of Complex, Ill-Specified Problems **Profit Drivers:** High Fees. Low Leverage, Referral of Work to Others
Low degree of client contact.	**Pharmacist** **Key Skill:** Supervision of Low-Cost Delivery Team **Profit Drivers:** High Leverage, Established Methodologies	**Brain Surgeon** **Key Skill:** Creative, Innovative Solutions to One-of-a-Kind Problems **Profit Drivers:** Premium Fees, Modest Leverage

Who Makes Most?

It is not immediately clear which kind of practice is the most profitable. While Psychotherapists may command the highest rate per hour, they might still earn the lowest income, since if there is little or no leverage, all profit derives only from their personal efforts—and there are only so many hours in a day, and so many days in a year. On the other hand, even in an intense fee-sensitive marketplace, the Pharmacist could make the highest per-partner profit by establishing low-cost delivery procedures and supervising a large volume of transactions.

As Figure 13.3 shows, while rates tend to increase as you move up and to the right, leverage tends to decline in the same directions. The greatest profit will come to those who can find the right mixture of rate and leverage.

This reasoning shows the importance of examining profitability on a fully costed, per-partner basis for each transaction. Some firms try to apply measures like *realization rates* (i.e., percent of standard fees obtained) to judge the profitability of all areas of practice. That this is misleading should be obvious from this analysis.

It is literally meaningless to complain about a Pharmacist's low realization or rates. They are by definition low—he or she is making aspirin! The key question that should be posed to the Pharmacist is

FIGURE 13.3

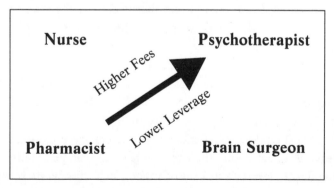

whether or not he or she knows how to leverage and thereby lower the cost of delivery.

Similarly, it would be nonsense to worry about how personally "chargeable" the Pharmacist is. A high-cost (and high-priced) partner in the pharmacy does not make the most money by personally making the aspirin. Instead, he or she should aim to supervise a large number of more-junior (less costly) people who will be highly utilized (i.e., chargeable).

All four kinds of providers can be equally profitable, especially if measured on a per-partner (or per-owner) basis, each using different mixtures of rate and leverage to achieve profitability.

In principle, all four kinds of providers can be equally profitable, especially if measured on a per-partner (or per-owner) basis, each using different mixtures of rate and leverage to achieve profitability. In fact, in the real world the two most consistently profitable practices are Nursing and Brain Surgery. This may be seen by contrasting these practices with their counterparts.

The pharmacy business is extremely fee-sensitive, and the only way to make high profits is to be extremely good at reducing the cost of delivery. Few professional firms rate themselves highly at this and, accordingly, do not make excellent profits in this area of practice.

However, if clients can be found who want not only good execution but also ongoing counseling (i.e., Nursing), then it will be possible to command a slightly higher fee for the interpersonal interaction the client wants. Compared to the Pharmacist, the Nurse can charge higher fees with little, if any, sacrifice of leverage. Nursing *should* be a more profitable business.

The converse logic applies to the Psychotherapists. Although they usually command premium fees, a high percentage of the work is conducted in the client's presence, and it will be hard to employ much, if any, leverage. However, if some part of the work (for example the investigative or analytical portion) can be conducted in the professional's back room, then greater leverage can be obtained at no sacrifice to fee levels. The Brain Surgeon can thus be more directly profitable (per partner) than the Psychotherapist.

The Need to Focus

The categorization scheme used here does not define whole disciplines, but rather different market segments. For example, many clients for a service like auditing may seek out a Pharmacist—the work, in their view, being mostly programmatic and performed with little need for ongoing client contact. However, other audit clients may require (and request) extensive diagnosis, and want a great deal of ongoing client interaction. They may seek a provider with demonstrated nursing or psychotherapy skills and methodologies. Which box you are in is determined less by the profession you practice than by the market segments you are trying to serve.

And therein lies the problem! Suppose that you are a highly skilled tax practitioner who handles complex, frontier tax problems through creative, innovative thinking (i.e., you are a Brain Surgeon). A client comes along who wants to get some basic tax forms completed, to ensure compliance with all tax laws. Since this is your client, it's a tax problem—and, since you're a tax provider, it is tempting to conclude that you're the perfect person to help the client.

Wrong! As a Brain Surgeon, you are probably high-priced, and your key talents are creativity and complex problem-solving. However, completing tax forms and ensuring compliance is a Pharmacy job; it is not work for a Brain Surgeon. A Brain Surgeon may have the tendency to treat all problems as if they require brain surgery: The client says "I'd like to buy some aspirin," and the Brain Surgeon replies "Sure! But first, get on the operating table so we can investigate and find out whether it's aspirin you really need!" There was perhaps a time when clients would accept this kind of treatment from their outside professionals, but it is not so today.

(Of course, the opposite problem is equally unacceptable. If a client says "I have a unique bet-your-company problem," it is not very sensible to respond by saying "Let us show you our established methodology based on years of solving identical problems!")

Even if the Brain Surgeon recognizes the need to treat a problem as an aspirin job, it would still be a misallocation of resources for that person to do it, since low-cost, methodology-driven activities are not his or her key talents. In fact, everyone will lose if you, as the Brain Surgeon, do it yourself: The client will not get low cost, you will be underutilizing your talents (and will probably find the work dull), and your junior staff will be denied the opportunity to perform work that, while old hat for you, might be interesting and skill-building for them.

It is common in all professions to see the clients' aspirin needs being served by off-duty Brain Surgeons, so that they can stay busy (i.e., chargeable).

Unfortunately, it is common in all professions to see the clients' aspirin needs being served by off-duty Brain Surgeons, so that they can stay busy (i.e., chargeable). Once in a while, it's OK for this to happen, but the Brain Surgeon is unlikely to sustain the skills and reputation that go with the job if he or she spends too much time making aspirin.

What this analysis points out is that while it may be acceptable for a *firm* to be a "full-service hospital" with capabilities to meet a broad range of client needs, it is not acceptable for individual professionals to try to do so. It is highly unlikely that any one individual will excel simultaneously at *all* the virtues of efficiency, creativity, counseling, and diagnosis.

Individuals, if they are to build a career, must become excellent at something specific: It is not enough to be "pretty good" at a wide range of things. Individuals must decide what kind of practitioner they want to be, and focus on building the essential skill that is required for that kind of practice.

Which Should I Choose?

In most professions there is an unfortunate tendency to consider some types of providers as having higher status than others. For example, many professionals have a self-image of being Brain Surgeons, and they value this role more highly than any other. It is also historically true that many clients treated their outsider providers like Brain Surgeons, regardless of the true nature of the problem. There was a time when clients said "I don't understand or want to understand the details of what you do— just take care of me and my problems, and I'll pay your bill!"

> **It is highly unlikely that any one individual will excel simultaneously at *all* the virtues of efficiency, creativity, counseling, and diagnosis.**

This is not an accurate description of today's marketplace. Today's clients are sophisticated buyers. They increasingly understand the differences between and among their aspirin, surgery, counseling, and diagnostic needs, and are ever more willing to shop differently when looking for providers to meet these separate needs. They no longer want elite generalists who will treat each problem as if it were brain surgery. They want specialists who can deliver the specific benefit required by the specific job at hand.

While brain surgery is the traditional self-image of many professions, the harsh reality is that it probably represents a very small percentage of the total fees paid in any profession. Of course, it is also true in real health care, where surgeons may be the most glamorous providers, yet they represent a tiny fraction of the health-care needs of society.

Two trends suggest where the bulk of the market lies. First, clients are buying fewer services as if their problems were totally unique. Instead, they more and more frequently want to tap into a firm's accumulated experience and methodologies, in order to benefit from the efficiencies that come from dealing with providers who have done it before. Accordingly, they are buying less brain surgery and more aspirin.

Second, clients are increasingly reluctant to say to their professionals "You take care of things and report back when it's all done." More and more, clients want to be involved in the process—or, at a minimum, be kept informed of their options and up-to-date on progress, and assisted in understanding what is going on, and why.

The bulk of the market is moving toward nursing (established, proven procedures with high client contact) and away from brain surgery.

From these two trends, we can conclude that the bulk of the market is moving toward nursing (established, proven procedures with high client contact) and away from brain surgery. As reflected by the amount of price competition in most professions, the pharmacy also represents a high percentage of fees. While critical, the role of Psychotherapist is not a high-volume area. It is filled with those few individuals who have sufficiently earned their clients' trust and confidence so that, whenever the client has a problem, the Psychotherapist is called in to prescribe what is needed.

Practitioners in these four areas lead very different lives. The choice of which area to practice in depends not only on profitability and market size, but also on how one wishes to spend his or her working life.

Professionals in charge of a pharmacy must enjoy supervising others, and must also enjoy *selling* aspirin: If you can't bring in the volume, there's no point in building a leveraged support structure beneath you. Nurses have to enjoy patiently explaining their discipline to lay people, and dealing with the concerns of nervous, worried clients.

Brain surgeons must thrive on the challenge of staying at the intellectual frontier of their field and working continually to both earn and deserve their premium fees. Psychotherapists must find fulfillment in the high-wire act of diagnosing and solving complex, unique problems during interaction with their clients. It should be clear that each of these fields attracts different kinds of personalities.

Is There a Career Path?

Saying that individuals must focus on or specialize in one of these areas in order to develop superior levels of the skill required by each type of practice does not mean that there is no chance of changing as one's career develops. In fact, there are traditionally well-established career paths at most professional firms.

Most professional firms put new entry-level people to work in the pharmacy first, so they can learn the key technical skills of their profession. As time progresses, people usually move in one of two directions, following either the technical career path to Brain Surgeon or the client-contact career path to Nurse.

Psychotherapists have tended to evolve from the more creative Nurses, although not all Nurses can make the transition to being accepted as the client's prime diagnostician. While it is possible for Brain Surgeons to become Psychotherapists, it is more rare. Unless a professional learns the basic client-contact skills early in his or her career, they are difficult to develop later.

This traditional approach to career development (often called *paying your dues*) is increasingly under attack. Consider the pharmacy service. Under the traditional career model, the aspirin is being made by professionals temporarily working in the pharmacy, serving their time until they are promoted to a higher-level service. This method of having the aspirin made by "Brain Surgeons in training" is not entirely aligned with the clients' interests.

Unlike the Brain Surgeon firm, which can afford to hire only the best and brightest from the top schools, a focused pharmacy practice would appropriately view these as the wrong people to bring in. Not only do they command higher salaries, but their superior intellect may be inappropriate for the service the pharmacy is trying to provide. If a firm's business is making hamburgers, it will not want to hire people who are dreaming of the day they can leave and become *cordon bleu* chefs. It will want and need people who are excited about hamburgers.

A focused pharmacy practice would be able to hire people without a formal education in its *specific* area, since smart people can learn to apply well-defined methodologies and tools. Training and development would be structured and formal, to ensure that new people can learn quickly to apply the firm's established methodologies. (This is exactly what is happening in some management consulting firms who now hire people with degrees in such diverse fields as anthropology and liberal arts.)

Employees in the pharmacy would *not* be promised a fast-track promotion and career path. In fact, there would be no traditional up-or-out policy. (This latter point is one reason why the Big-6 accounting firms, increasingly realizing that much of their business is pharmacy, have recently moved away from such policies.)

The nursing practice requires capable people who not only are able to apply methodologies, but also are able to work well with clients. One common approach is to hire individuals who have prior industry experience working in client environments, in order to maximize the chance that these individuals can empathize with the client situation.

Other approaches are possible. For one law-firm client, I helped develop a recruiting process to screen for counseling skills. Every candidate who obtained a final interview was asked to explain his or her favorite law-school course to one of the firm's secretaries. In this way, the firm was able to distinguish between those candidates who had a personal mastery of their field, and those who also had the ability to communicate their expertise to a layperson.

Naturally, the Brain Surgeon practice would hire the best and brightest, and, since such people are eminently mobile and marketable, offer a fast-track, up-or-out career system. Here, training would be significantly less formal, relying largely upon the traditional apprenticeship model of learning by working with mentors.

Finally, Psychotherapists hire very rarely and selectively, and almost never at the entry level. Such practices tend to rely (appropriately) on seasoned senior hires—often those with significant industry experience.

Another aspect of firm management that differs between and among types of practices is ownership. For both Psychotherapy and Brain Surgery practices, the value that the firm renders is embedded in the specific skills of the mobile and marketable individuals who make up the firm. Accordingly, to retain such people, firms must be relatively open with their ownership. They must either be partnerships, or corporations that provide easy access to equity for senior people.

> **For both Psychotherapy and Brain Surgery practices, the value that the firm renders is embedded in the specific skills of the mobile and marketable individuals who make up the firm. Accordingly, to retain such people, firms must be relatively open with their ownership.**

In contrast, the nursing and pharmacy practices have more of their value embedded in the systems and procedures of the firm, and are less dependent on the individual skills of individual people. Such practices can be—and often are—wholly-owned corporations with limited ownership. Some form of profit sharing, rather than full-equity participation, is sufficient to retain key players. For a summary of these "people issues," see Figure 13.4.

FIGURE 13.4

	Standardized Process	Customized Process
High degree of client contact.	**Nurse** ✚ **Hiring:** Interpersonal skills stressed **Training:** Formal, including role-plays of client situations **Promotion:** Limited if remain in this box **Ownership:** Profit sharing, but little equity sharing	**Psychothcrapist** 🕐🛏 **Hiring:** Very selective, experienced experts with industry experience **Training:** Experiential, if any **Promotion:** Up-or-out in short time-frame **Ownership:** Broadly shared
Low degree of client contact.	**Pharmacist** ℞ **Hiring:** Paraprofessionals and other low-cost resources **Training:** Formal, structured **Promotion:** Few opportunities **Ownership:** Closely held	**Brain Surgeon** ✂ **Hiring:** Best and brightest from top schools **Training:** Informal, apprenticeship **Promotion:** Fast-track, up-or-out **Ownership:** Partnership or "open equity"

Marketing

Like all other business issues, marketing and client relations differ significantly among the practice types described here. In a pharmacy practice, the client is buying the comfort, security, and reassurance provided by the firm's systems, procedures, and training. Accordingly, a pharmacy would market *the firm itself,* rather than specific individuals. Significant effort would be expended upon creating a brand name, and upon such mass-marketing tools as direct mail and brochures. Even advertising would find a place in the marketing mix.

Nursing is more of a relationship business, and a solid reputation for client service skills (whether individual or institutional, but more likely the former) is the key to marketplace success. Word-of-mouth and referrals play an important role in winning Nurses their future business.

Psychotherapists and Brain Surgeons need to stress the reputation and skills of individual practitioners rather than those of the firm itself. (This is reflected in the familiar slogan of clients, "I hire lawyers, not law firms.") Marketing is heavily customized for both types of practitioner, with a strong emphasis on word-of-mouth referrals.

The Psychotherapist would tend to have fewer, deeper relations with selected key clients, while the Brain Surgeon's business would be more transactional. Accordingly, the Psychotherapist is more likely to have an in-depth knowledge of a particular client sector, while the Brain Surgeon would focus more on building an outstanding technical reputation.

Summary

The four types of practice described here are amazingly different. One could go on and on comparing the needs of each type of practice. I can't resist offering one more: The question of *managerial style.* The pharmacy, with its high-leverage, familiar, methodology-driven work and fee sensitivity, clearly requires a style that emphasizes discipline, measurement, order, and clear job structures. What is truly needed here is a management style which is similar to that used in a well-organized military operation.

However, a group of psychotherapy practitioners cannot be managed this way, since the discipline will admit to few established procedures, every client problem is different, and value is not rendered in the office, but rather in contact with the client. The only style that would be effective here would be that of a participative and consultative player–coach.

If these practices are so different, then there clearly is only one mistake that can be made: running the whole hospital in the same way. Yet—of course—this is exactly what many firms do. "Consulting is consulting," they say; or "Tax is tax." Well, they're not! If you don't understand what business you are really in, you are likely to manage your practice in dysfunctional ways (such as having the Brain Surgeons making aspirin). What you need to understand is not only what you want to sell, but what your clients want to buy.

> There clearly is only one mistake that can be made: running the whole hospital in the same way. Yet—of course—this is exactly what many firms do.

Very frequently I encounter firms whose core problem is that their practitioners want to be Brain Surgeons, but they are in a marketplace that wants to buy Nurses. There's no dishonor in being a Nurse, and it's perfectly valid to want to be a Brain Surgeon. But what is *not* acceptable is pretending—acting like Brain Surgeons when your clients want Nurses.

Either go out and generate some real brain-surgery business, or start restructuring your firm around the key skills needed by your nursing clients. Either path will work. Living with the mismatch will not.

I have tried to stress that the primary issue in this analysis is about the individual—who, I believe, must decide what he or she wants to be. A firm, particularly a large one, *can* afford to have practitioners in all of these areas (i.e., be a full-service hospital). However, doing this well is not a trivial task. It requires organizing specialist groups, understanding how each needs to be managed, running each of them differently, and ensuring appropriate collaboration (and cross-referrals) between them.

For example: On large, complex transactions, it is often the case that *part* of the job may require either some or all of these types of work, and a well-functioning hospital could serve clients best if it were able to refer appropriate portions of the client's assignment to the appropriate specialist.

That is at least the theory. In *reality,* large firms encounter two problems that prevent this ideal solution. First, they often are not organized into specialist groups as defined here, but rather into generic discipline groups (i.e., the tax department). Getting the pharmacy work handled by pharmacy specialists remains a problem. Second, the ideal solution implies that the professionals handling the work will willingly hand over portions of the task to others—something that, alas, does not always happen. The ideal solution remains just that: an ideal.

There is one final issue for the full-service firm: market reputation. If your clientele knows you primarily as a superior dispenser of aspirin, how does that image affect your ability to win a reputation for being their Brain Surgeon or Psychotherapist? Is it really possible to have one brand name that excels in creating a reputation for creativity, low cost, counseling, and diagnosis—*all at once?* I doubt it.

For most firms, as well as for individuals, there is great power in knowing precisely who you are, precisely what you specialize in, and precisely which client needs you intend to excel at.

What kind of provider are *you?*

14

MANAGING YOUR CLIENT'S PROJECTS

I have moderated many client panels where the main message from the clients to the professionals has been: "When we turn over an engagement to you, we don't just get *you*—we get your entire engagement team. And we want to know that you are truly managing the total assignment, and everyone involved with it. Obviously we want your personal skill and attention. But, just as important, we want you to actively *manage* the totality of the transaction."

Clients overwhelmingly report that many of the professional firms they deal with do *not* have internal systems in place that would allow them to manage engagements properly. Clients know this by the firm's inability to provide (on request) progress reports, budget expenditures against plan, and other forms of work and cost updates. Clients also readily perceive that many partners are more interested in their own

> Obviously we want your personal skill and attention. But, just as important, we want you to actively *manage* the totality of the transaction."

involvement (and billable hours) than they are in supervising the rest of the team.

Most firms are vigorous in collecting financial information on the performance of individuals or groups of individuals (e.g., in profit centers or practice areas). However, in a professional firm the most important unit of analysis is neither the individual nor the practice group. The most important perspective from which to understand the economics of practice is at the level of *the engagement* (or deal, transaction, assignment, or matter). *That* is what clients care about most!

> **The most important perspective from which to understand the economics of practice is at the level of *the engagement* (or deal, transaction, assignment, or matter). *That* is what clients care about most!**

In many professions, rising fee pressure and an increase in fixed-fee billing is forcing firms to reconsider their systems for the wise management of engagements. Obviously, if you have a fixed fee, profitability can come only from good cost management. This means having a reporting system which identifies as precisely as possible the costs incurred in conducting the engagement.

Engagement-Level P&L Statements

Regardless of how they price their services, all firms should produce fully costed profit-and-loss (P&L) statements for each engagement. Once developed, a database of profitability measurements per engagement will allow firms to examine which kinds of engagements are more or less profitable. It will prove to be an invaluable tool for directing practice-development efforts. Additionally, it would enable engagements of similar types to be compared, thus highlighting the opportunities for efficiency improvements. Further, a close analysis of engagement profitability would encourage wise decisions on the allocation of senior professional time, by clearly revealing which activities bring a greater or lesser return.

Engagement-level P&Ls can be more than a source of analytical information—they can also provide the basis for a productive *incentive* system. If engagement leaders are held accountable not only for revenues and write-offs, but also for the costs incurred in performing their transactions, they will be forced to give more attention to how engagements are staffed, how well junior professionals understand their tasks and are supervised, and how efficiently and effectively the total team works together.

Doing the Arithmetic

Customizing existing financial record-keeping software to produce an engagement-level P&L is usually not too difficult. In most systems there already exist computerized records of cash receipts by engagement, and—for each timekeeper on the engagement—both a record of hours logged and a standard billing rate. To make this a costing system, all that needs to be done is to change the billing-rate column into a cost column by entering the cost per hour of that timekeeper. (This entry usually needs to be done only once per year.) By doing so, you have both revenues and costs for the engagement, and can analyze it any way you want. One method of procedure is shown in Figure 14.1.

Figure 14.1 shows an engagement for which a total of $112,000 in time charges (valued at the firm's standard rates) were incurred, and a bill of $112,000 was successfully rendered and paid (for a realization rate of 100%).

From this cash receipt, we will first deduct the cost of junior professional time incurred on this assignment. For each junior professional, we take the total of his or her annual salary plus fringe benefits, and divide that total by a standard (target) number of billable hours—the

FIGURE 14.1

Summary of Hypothetical Firm's P&L

	Overall Firm Results		This Engagement	
Revenue	$63.9M	100%	$112K	100%
Junior Professional salaries	$14.1M	22%	$19K	17%
Gross contribution	$49.8M	78%	$93K	83%
Other expenses				
Overhead	$30.4M	47.6%	—	—
Partner cost	$19.4M	30.3%	$41K	37%
Contribution/ Partner cost (i.e., return on value of partner time)	($49.8/$19.4)	$2.57	($93/$41)	$2.27

Note: In a corporate firm, reference to partners would be inappropriate. As pointed out in the text, there are two modifications that are possible. Either the term *senior professional* can be used (thus calculating a return on senior professional time, which is a valuable calculation), and/or the costs of senior professional time could be *subtracted from* the gross contribution (instead of divided into it), and the resulting net contribution be compared to the fee for the job, in order to derive a margin percentage.

same target number for each junior professional. This gives us a cost per billable hour for each junior professional. When multiplied by the number of hours spent by that junior professional on this engagement, we get the total costs incurred on this assignment by that junior professional. Repeating this for each junior professional (and paraprofessional) on the engagement yields our total nonpartner labor cost. (Assume that this is $19,000 in this case.)

If we deduct this sum from the cash receipts (and also deduct any cash disbursements made on behalf of the client that were not reimbursed), we obtain the gross contribution. In this case, assuming no disbursements, it is $112K minus $19K, or $93,000.

This $93,000 is the amount available to cover overhead and partner profit. To turn this contribution figure into a pure profit number, we would need a method for allocating overhead expenses to each matter, which is complicated (and *controversial*); let's for the moment deal with the gross contribution figure of $93,000. Is this a good profit? It is impossible to say without examining how much partner (or senior professional) time had to be invested in order to yield that $93,000. How then *do* we account for partner time?

My preferred approach is to use the latest available partner-compensation numbers, and to divide each partner's compensation by the same (target) number of billable hours. For example, if our target billable hours for partners is 1,600 hours and we have two partners earning $320,000 and $160,000 respectively, their cost to the firm will be calculated as $200 and $100 per billable hour respectively. Thus the higher-paid partner shows up (appropriately) as costing the firm more per billable hour than the lower-paid partner.

We examine each partner who contributed to the engagement, and multiply his or her hours on the engagement by that partner's cost per hour. To be kind, we will *not* refer to the total as a cost, but as a number reflecting how much of the "partner equity" was invested in that engagement. Let's assume that this calculation shows that a total value of $41,000 of partner time (costed on the basis of total compensation) was invested in this engagement.

Now we can ask: Did the firm get a good return on the value of the partner time invested in this engagement? We divide the gross contribution ($93,000) by the partner investment ($41,000) and get a ratio of 227%. This appears high: Be sure to understand what it represents! Remember that the gross contribution must cover *both* partner compensation *and* overhead. The ratio of contribution to partner investment must be at least 100% to cover the partner's (latest year) compensation. How much higher must it be to cover the overhead as well?

A brief look at the firm's aggregate (annual) financials will yield the answer. As may be seen in Figure 14–1, each dollar of partner compensation must generate $2.57 of gross contribution ($49.8M/$19.4M) if overhead is to be met and partner compensation merely maintained. It must generate *more* than $2.57 if partner compensation is to rise. So, the target for this firm is for the ratio of gross contribution to partner compensation to meet or exceed 257%.

The concept of gross contribution may seem strange (combining as it does overhead and profit), but it allows us to analyze an individual client matter simply. By using this method, the firm can get as close as is possible to a professional firm's traditional profit measure—profit per partner—without incurring the troublesome task of allocating overhead costs to individual assignments.

The costs that *can* be allocated, reliably and unarguably, to a particular matter—in particular the cost of nonpartner timekeepers—are allocated. The rest are left as general overhead. (The effect of this approach is equivalent to charging each assignment with the firm's average overhead cost ratio. Once a firm has established the principle and practice of engagement-level P&Ls, it may want to consider exploring more fine-tuned methods of allocating overhead expenses to engagements.)

This calculation reveals that the specific engagement we are examining, with a return of 227%, is slightly below the firm's target profitability. The firm is recovering its standard billing rates (the ratio of receipts to standard value of time billed was 100%), which finding would lead most firms to define it as a profitable engagement. But it has a low contribution per partner-dollar invested. Something is askew! It's very common to discover that engagements previously thought profitable turn out to yield a low return on partner (or senior professional) time, and vice versa. The explanation is simple: Achieving a good rate is *not* the same thing as achieving a good profit per partner—and the latter is a *lot* more important!

A brief comment needs to made for those professional firms structured as corporations rather than partnerships. The logic used above still applies to them, but with some minor modifications. First, it is just as essential for them to have a costing system at the assignment, engagement, or project level. However, they may choose not to calculate a "return on senior professional time," as previously shown, but instead deduct the cost of senior professional time from the gross contribution. This move obtains a net contribution, which can then be compared to the fee for the job, and thereby derive an overall margin percentage. This is an adequate substitution for the "return" ratio used above.

Using the Reports

What could be wrong with our sample engagement? The possible answers are many, illustrating that the power of this tool lies less in producing formulaic answers than in causing productive discussions to result. Possible issues arising are:

• Could this engagement have been more profitable if we had used a less highly paid partner? Is this partner too valuable to be doing this kind of work?

• Could the engagement have been conducted with the same quality, but by using a little less partner time and a little more (well-supervised) junior professional time, resulting in a better return on the partner time?

• By way of converse argument, should we have used less junior professional time and more partner time, but charged more for this transaction? Note that the arithmetical calculation is not biased toward either high *or* low leverage. A low-leverage engagement can generate an excellent return on partner time invested, as long as the fees received are high.

• Could we have saved time (and cost) anywhere in this assignment and still billed an amount the client considered fair? (Note that the arithmetic shown in Figure 14–1 makes no assumption about the basis for billing—it simply compares revenues and costs, regardless of how the firm bills for its work.)

• Is this kind of engagement consistently below our target return? Should we either develop lower-cost methods of doing this kind of transaction, or withdraw from the market?

• Is there a good reason to accept below-average profitability in this case? Is this an assignment for an otherwise profitable (or strategically important) client for which this lower return should be accepted as a sensible investment? Or is this perhaps our first assignment in a new market we are trying to penetrate?

The key point here is that a simple calculation of engagement-profitability statement causes numerous questions to be raised that would never have surfaced had the firm stuck to traditional performance measures. Most firms would have said "Hmm, 100% realization—not bad! Carry on!" This new measure will cause the discussions that clients want ("How are you staffing my engagement? Who is worrying about the total budget?") and the discussions that firms must have if they are to succeed ("How do we reduce the cost of doing this kind of transaction? How much should I do, and how much can I usefully delegate and still get quality and productivity?")

Implementation Details

There are, of course, numerous questions raised by the approach described previously. Many firms ask "Why do you divide everybody's salary by a standard number of hours and not their actual hours?" The answer is that if you had someone with a low number of hours, dividing the salary by the personal hours would result in an extremely high hourly cost, and no one would ever want that person on their engagement. The busiest people (with a low effective hourly cost) would be in even greater demand, and the least busy would be in least demand. This would be perverse.

A related question is "Doesn't a standard cost system ignore the fact that if we utilize a junior professional an extra 500 hours, all that extra work is cost-free and goes straight to the bottom line?" Yes, the system ignores this—and for a purpose. If you want to make money by working the junior professionals harder—fine, but that's a completely separate issue. It has nothing to do with whether or not you are staffing and managing your engagements well.

Working your junior professionals harder will mean taking on more engagements, and if that's what you want to do, OK! That's making money by focusing on getting more production. But be careful: Don't confuse that issue with those of productivity and efficiency. Increasing production is not the same thing as increasing productivity. The former is a short-term tactic, the latter essential for long-run competitiveness.

The next objection heard is "Won't this system encourage partners to record fewer hours in order to raise the apparent return on their time?" Obviously, if taken on a stand-alone basis, this incentive might exist. However, the key point is that engagement profitability is not a substitute for other control systems of the firm, but a *complement* to them. The firm must still track billable hours (or utilization) and, by so doing, will readily uncover any such games-playing.

A more worthy objection has to do with overheads. "If I use fewer junior professionals, why do I have to meet a target based on the firm's aggregate overhead? By using fewer junior professionals, I require less of the firm's overhead costs in the form of space, training, and so on." In point of fact, a fully costed system including the allocation of overhead costs *would* make sense, but there are at least two arguments against *starting* with such a system.

First, the experience of many of my clients shows that agreeing on an overhead allocation scheme can be extremely controversial and, more to the point, rarely changes the results significantly. (Don't take my word for it—try it yourself!) Second, it cannot be stressed enough that the results of engagement-profitability reports are not intended to be used in a formulaic way, but as a means to initiate discussions and thinking about efficiency and productivity. Holding partners accountable for overhead allocations simply gives them a reason to dispute the validity of the results, since they cannot control overhead directly.

Some firms will encounter another implementation difficulty if they track cash receipts only at the client level and cannot attribute them to specific engagements (if payment was for a number of engagements). However, most clients prefer bills that clearly show "how much for each transaction," so adjusting the firm's systems to keep track of each engagement separately serves the client as well as the firm.

Extra Benefits

Many firms have found that an engagement-profitability system, once installed, has some extra benefits. It makes it easy to manage unbilled work-in-process (WIP) and overdue accounts receivable (A/R). By charging the engagement P&L an interest cost (based on the firm's borrowing rate) for all unbilled WIP and uncollected A/R, you can reveal immediately that if these are excessive, then the profitability of the engagement is reduced. By accounting for the costs of WIP and A/R at the engagement level, these costs are highlighted in real time.

If the partner is held *accountable* for engagement profitability, there will be a keenly felt incentive to manage these items. More than a few firms have found that a significant behavioral change among partners resulted when this approach was adopted. A model showing an engagement P&L reflecting these factors is shown in Figure 14.2.

It is possible to use the costing system to accomplish strategic objectives. For example, one firm with which I have worked adjusts the cost-per-hour figures assigned to engagement P&Ls for junior professionals who need to be trained, and for those being rotated through different departments or offices—thus providing an incentive for partners to employ these "less-productive" resources while still achieving firm goals.

A similar effect has been achieved in those professional firms (such as audit firms) that have a significant seasonality to their work—where professionals are overstretched at peak periods, and systematically underutilized at other times of the year. For decades, audit firms have preached to their partners that they should work with their

FIGURE 14.2
Engagement-Level Profitability Reporting

Net Cash Receipts
minus
Cost of nonpartner time (Nonpartner hours × cost per hour of each person)
minus
Uncollected disbursements
minus
Cost of unbilled time (Value of hours not billed within 30 days × cost of borrowing)
minus
Accounts receivable cost (Bills outstanding over 30 days × cost of borrowing)
equals
Gross Contribution
divided by
Partner Investment in the matter (Partner hours × cost per hour of the partner)
equals
Return on Partner Investment

Note: See Figure 13.1 for modifications necessary if "partnership" terminology is not used.

clients to try to reschedule some of the work from peak periods into underutilized periods. Their exhortations usually fall on deaf ears.

However, with the introduction of engagement-level profitability measures it became simple to employ seasonal costing, so that a junior professional used at peak periods was an expensive resource, but the same person used in off-peak periods was a low-cost one. In the effort to improve the engagement profitability for which they were personally accountable, partners now had a more personal and direct incentive to shift work out of the peak periods—and dramatic results were achieved.

Rewarding and Recognizing Supervision

The successful implementation of engagement-level P&Ls requires that for every engagement there is a clearly designated "supervising partner." This role has long been neglected in both the management and the reward systems of professional firms. The supervising partner doesn't have to be either the one who brought in the work, or the one who logs the most hours to the engagement (although he or she *may* be one of these individuals). Instead, the system described in this chapter recognizes that *managing* an engagement is a critical role to be performed and one that requires critical skill.

It is time that minding—*the wise management of engagements*—be restored to its rightful place high on the list of things a firm must do well to compete in today's marketplace.

Remember the old litany of "finders, minders, and grinders"? Too many firms have excellent systems to track and reward finding and grinding, but no system to measure or reward minding. It is time that minding—*the wise management of engagements*—be restored to its rightful place high on the list of things a firm must do well to compete in today's marketplace.

15

WHY MERGE?

The track record of mergers among professional firms has not been impressive. Although few mergers have proven disastrous, just as few have clearly delivered competitive benefits. Mergers *can be* successful—it's just that few of them *have been*.

> Mergers *can be* successful—it's just that few of them *have been*. For a merger to confer a competitive advantage, it must create an additional benefit for clients, not just for the firms involved.

For a merger to confer a competitive advantage, it must create an additional benefit for clients, not just for the firms involved. This simple principle seems obvious, but is not always observed.

For example, many firms justify mergers on the grounds that "We can refer clients to each other and increase our revenues." True enough, but that could be done *without* merging. What added value do the clients get from intrafirm referrals as opposed to referrals between firms? Obviously not much. Although referrals do flow between merged firms (even if not in the quantities dreamed of), neither firm can be said to be more valuable to clients (i.e., competitively stronger) thereafter than before.

What might be the benefits to clients of a professional firm merger? Consider five kinds of such that I refer to variously as the *menu, bulk, dots, alchemy,* and *crisis* mergers.

The Menu Merger

The *menu* merger attempts to create a competitive advantage by adding additional services to the firm's service offerings, thus aiming to provide clients with a broader range through effective cross-selling. Does this work? Maybe—but here's a simple test question: Historically speaking, how successful have your premerger cross-selling efforts been? If you've got a good track record of cross-selling (which few firms have), then go for it. If not, then what makes you think you'll be good at cross-selling the new stuff when you haven't been able to do that with the old stuff? The "one-stop-shopping supermarket" approach has been tried in numerous businesses and professions, and has been discredited almost everywhere.

However, maybe some of *your* clients would appreciate it. The simplest way of finding out is to go to the horse's mouth and ask. Select a group of the clients to whom you think these new services would most appeal. Invite the group to dinner, and say "This is confidential, but we're thinking of bringing on board some people with additional specialties." (You don't have to tell them it's a merger.) Then continue with "What's your reaction? Would you find this appealing? Would you use us in these new areas?" You don't have to accept all of their answers as gospel, but you'll get a good temperature reading on the market reaction to this initiative. It is amazing how infrequently firms conduct this simple activity, even when contemplating transactions involving millions of dollars and hundreds of people.

Notice that there are really *two* issues here—as there are in *all* mergers: whether clients would value the benefit you seek to create (in this case, having an expanded range of services), and whether a merger is the best way to accomplish it.

There are really *two* issues here—as there are in *all* mergers: whether clients would value the benefit you seek to create, and whether a merger is the best way to accomplish it.

The Bulk Merger

The *bulk* merger is based on the theory that you have to be big to be credible. It is defined as a merger between similar firms in the same locations, and the theory behind it is that by getting bigger, the firm will be better able to compete. A big firm, it is believed, has the resources which enable it to handle the kinds of large assignments or projects that a smaller firm perhaps can't (or might not be able to convince the marketplace that it can). It is also at least hoped that a big firm will have a greater market presence, and so will be included more regularly on clients' lists of professional firms to be considered.

It cannot be denied that size helps in marketing. However, it is a poor substitute for it. Market credibility, and being invited to propose with great frequency, are goals that can be achieved through effective marketing. Merging to achieve market credibility is like using a sledgehammer to crack a nut. Firms that are interested in bulk mergers are, in effect, saying "We don't know how to get better, so we'll get bigger, because size helps—a little."

Of course, increasing size does not necessarily lead to greater profitability for professional firms. *Few* of the things that determine a firm's success—client service, innovation, productivity enhancements, collaboration—are critically dependent on size. Firms can, and should, be working on these topics anyway, long before they look to size to solve their problems. No client will be fooled into thinking that when two medium-size "OK" firms merge, and become a giant "OK" firm, the clients are going to be better served.

On a per-partner basis, a small firm can be as profitable as a larger one, if not more so. The key to improving profitability in a professional firm is to improve the quality of the practice—obtaining better-paying, more-leveraged, high-fee engagements. If this can be done without scale (through marketing, innovation, client service, or creativity), then size is optional. Conversely, if bulking up just means more of the low-fee, less-leveraged projects, then profitability will probably decline. As the old saying goes: "Volume is vanity—profits are sanity."

The Dots Merger

The *dots* merger describes combinations of similar firms in different geographic regions. Here there is an attempt to gain a competitive advantage by adding locations, thereby offering *global, national,* or *regional* coverage.

There clearly would be a client need for the multilocation firm if the client had work that needed to be conducted *simultaneously* in multiple jurisdictions (as, for example, much audit work for multinational companies requires). The ability to handle such multilocation work provides an inarguable rationale for end-to-end mergers. However, the vast majority of client work in multilocation firms does *not* require this kind of simultaneous, joint activity between locations.

Why, then, would a client want its provider to be multisite? There might be cases where a client would prefer to deal with one firm for particular kinds of work, but might not want to spend time and money flying professionals around. Or, a client may well want its regular domestic firm to have an overseas office for some ongoing business.

Of course, nothing appeals equally to all clients—or prospects. Some of your clients will find what you are planning attractive, and others will be indifferent about it. It is important to know *specific*

> **Nothing appeals equally to all clients—or prospects. You need to research (and confirm) which individual clients will benefit from your planned initiative.**

clients' needs up front. You need to research (and confirm) which individual clients will benefit from your planned initiative.

Many mergers have been motivated by a misguided desire to be everywhere. Opening or acquiring an office to balance out the map in the firm's brochure isn't justification enough, although it is remarkable how often this ends up being the prevailing rationale.

My experience is that few clients consider geographic coverage to be a significant consideration when selecting a professional firm, except in those rare instances when there is work to be performed simultaneously in multiple jurisdictions. On matters of any importance, the clients want to identify the individual(s) who can serve them best, rather than simply taking whoever is assigned to their professional firm's remote location. They generally believe that they can choose for themselves the right experts in different practice areas.

I remember interviewing a Dallas, Texas, client on behalf of a Big-6 accounting firm that was trying to promote its international tax services. She said "I wish these firms would stop coming in and showing me a map of the world with all their dots on it, and thinking that's going to impress me. Treat me like a sensible adult. The fact that you have a partner in, say, Paris, to whom you can refer me if I have a French tax problem, adds zero value to me. I don't have difficulty finding a credible tax advisor in Paris. Intrafirm cross-referrals may be good for you, but they don't do anything for me unless you can show that I can derive extra benefit from using your person in that other location."

"What could that benefit be?" I asked. "Well," she said, "What I need is not so much international firms as international people. Give me someone here in Dallas who can talk sensibly about European Community law. People like that are relatively scarce, and hence valuable. Or convince me that your firm's standards of quality and service are so rigidly enforced that the mere fact that you are in partnership with this person guarantees me a high level of excellence and responsiveness. That has rarely been my experience—what you get from a firm depends on the individual you get in each location, and the fact that they were referred by a colleague guarantees nothing."

> **"What I need is not so much international firms as international people."**

What this indicates is that the mere existence of multiple locations is not worth much to clients. It's what you can *do* with your multiple locations that determines whether or not the geographic expansion benefits clients. For example, some geographic mergers *have* greatly enhanced firms' abilities to serve clients. They did this by enabling practitioners in specialized practice groups from multiple jurisdictions to meet regularly, collaborate on joint projects, share knowledge, and/or develop joint training, thereby enhancing the capabilities of the individual practitioner in each location. This is equivalent to creating "international people."

The activity that creates the merger benefit is the effective functioning of the multisite practice group.

The activity that creates the merger benefit is the effective functioning of the multisite practice group. Merger benefits can be brought to market if, and *only* if, new ways are found to collaborate to enhance capabilities. This teaches three important lessons.

First: Geographic merger benefits are most likely to occur at the practice-group level, rather than at the firm level.

Second: The capturing of merger benefits is primarily about creating new capabilities, and not primarily about marketing.

Third: The effects of a merger are almost always different for each practice area. What might appear to be one merger is in fact a series of separate mergers, as each practice group tries to wrestle with how it can create new capabilities by using its new combination.

The Alchemy Merger

The *alchemy* merger is based on the expectation of synergy. By merging, it is hoped, the firm will be able to create something new. Let's acknowledge immediately that this can be done. In fact, as difficult as it is to do well, *this* is the most powerful of all merger types. A perfect example of this approach is the creation of multidisciplinary practices. In those parts of the world where regulatory barriers do not exist, this movement is well-advanced and flourishing.

Take, for example, the entry of accounting firms into legal practice. If the lawyers working in these firms practice as stand-alone lawyers conducting a purely legal practice, there probably won't be much extra benefit to clients from the fact that they are owned by or associated with an accounting firm. They will be just one more law firm (albeit perhaps one managed a little better) in the marketplace. But it is a different story if the accounting firms start building legal expertise into their accounting, tax, and consulting practices.

Consulting and accounting firms advise companies on acquisitions, sales, joint ventures, initial public offerings, and a whole host of other big-ticket, complex deals. There is no business reason why they couldn't (and shouldn't) build an integrated legal component into their services in these areas, providing a soup-to-nuts service and eradicating the need for the outside law firms entirely. In fact, it's fairly obvious that—where regulations allow—the accounting firms are well on their way to doing just that.

An additional example is given by the many employee-benefit consulting firms that have traditionally provided design, analysis, and advice on benefit packages, but have often had to turn the work over to law firms in order to get plans registered, in compliance, filed, etc. In the future, with alchemy they could have the in-house capability to handle all aspects, and the flow of work to law firms could dry up.

Of course, it is not only the law firms that are under attack. They, too, can take the initiative. Many law firms (particularly in the United States) have successfully built multidisciplinary "alchemical" practices in such areas as health-care consulting, environmental consulting, international trade consulting, real-estate management consulting, economic research, and computer software development. Other alchemical approaches can be seen underway in the consulting market where corporate-strategy consultants are furiously trying to get more involved with implementation advice in addition to being information technology providers.

Ultimately, these initiatives will transform the competitive landscape upon which these firms compete. However, firms will not do so merely by bringing these different specialists in-house through merger or hiring. The key added-value (from the client's perspec-

> **The key added-value (from the client's perspective) will be the ability to design, coordinate, and integrate a variety of diverse specialists.**

tive) will be the ability to design, coordinate, and integrate a variety of diverse specialists. This will place significant stress on firms, as well as challenge their abilities to manage a beast completely different from the one they are used to.

Another way to think about this is to recognize that, on complex transactions, clients need a prime contractor who will take responsibility for the total job—including the management, coordination, and integration of a variety of technical-discipline specialists needed to take care of the various detailed issues (managerial, accounting, legal, financial, consulting, business strategy, and so on). The question, then, is "Who credibly possesses the project-management skills essential to be the prime contractor?" Many firms have merged or acquired their way to bringing multiple specialists in-house. Few have convinced the market that they have created (and can manage) a seamless, integrated service.

> **Many firms have merged or acquired their way to bringing multiple specialists in-house. Few have convinced the market that they have created (and can manage) a seamless, integrated service.**

The Crisis Merger

The *crisis* merger, one of the most common types, fits none of the previously described categories. It is based on the fact that the single greatest benefit derived from most professional-firm mergers is the creation of immense disruption within the merged firm(s). This disorder creates the conditions to make significant managerial changes that could not politically have been accomplished premerger—even if they were sensible and obvious then.

Most competitive benefits are obtained by improving a firm's approaches to such basics as client service, efficiency, innovation, skill development, resource allocation, and collaboration. However, making such improvements often requires significant changes in organization, accountabilities, measurement, and reporting systems—radical changes for which it is often hard to build consensus.

The merging of two firms throws all the cards up in the air. The newly merged firm *must* reexamine its organizational structure, its systems, and its choice of practice leaders and other managerial roles. Significant changes in how the practice is managed can be introduced during this mandatory review. Frequently, newly merged firms introduce new measurement and accountability systems for which it would have been impossible for either firm to obtain broad support or approval premerger.

> Frequently, newly merged firms introduce new measurement and accountability systems for which it would have been impossible for either firm to obtain broad support or approval premerger.

Another common merger benefit occurs when one of the merging firms has superior client-service characteristics, or better methodologies, or more-disciplined management. The combined entity results in these strong traits prevailing, and the weaker firm acquiring the superior practices of the stronger firm.

Of course, there is no reason why the weaker firm couldn't have implemented better practice approaches on its own—except that without a precipitating crisis event, the power to change is often absent. It is sad to report, but a large percentage of professional mergers I have observed have been driven by the need to create some form of crisis before significant changes could be made. It is important for firms to realize that the window of opportunity in making these changes is short—12 to 18 months. If revolutionary practices have not been introduced within that time frame, then the chance for radical change has usually been lost.

Lessons

In spite of the cynicism I have expressed here, I do believe that some mergers can be wise strategic moves for the right firms. The principles to observe are relatively few, and quite simple.

First, make sure that you focus on doing something that clients will value. This means that you should concentrate on the operational issues of creating new capabilities. *Don't* get seduced by the potential marketing benefits of mergers. If your merger allows you to have something new or better to offer the market, then the marketing of that additional capability will follow easily. If *all* merger benefits are marketing-related, be deeply skeptical.

Another good rule of thumb is to focus on acquiring talent rather than clients or client contacts. Because of the ephemeral nature of cross-selling opportunities, the values of the client relationships are a lot less certain than are the skills of the people. An acquisi-tion should be seen predominantly as a way of acquiring either talent or methodologies and tools, not clients. A merger is a long-term ac-tion, and you should therefore focus more on what it does for your balance sheet and assets, and a little less on what it does for your in-come statement.

Focus on acquiring talent rather than clients or client contacts.

It is often said that doing a professional-firm merger is like bring-ing in a very large number of lateral partners (together with their staffs) all at once. Amazingly, it is often the case that the due-dili-gence investigation done on an individual lateral-partner candidate exceeds in thoroughness that done when bringing in a whole firmful of them! Viewed this way, it is almost always smarter to raid and cherry-pick a small handful of key people to build a practice around, rather than merge with a whole firm. That way, you don't pay a pre-mium, and it's easier to integrate the new team into your way of doing things. It's slower, but definitely more trouble-free.

Firms must focus on the client-benefit issue as early as possible, preferably at the time the merger discussions first begin to be seri-ous. It is often sensible to give this task to individual practice groups, and ask them to come back with an action plan outlining how they intend to create new capabilities in a combined firm. Alas, this is rarely done. As soon as merger discussions start, joint strategy work is put on hold while the administrative detail of due diligence and merger negotiations takes place. Only after the deal is done is seri-ous thought given as to whether the joint-strategy hypothesis that prompted the merger idea can, in fact, be translated into reality. Before you do something as big and as serious as a merger, you need more than just a tentative hypothesis!

> A merger is a long-term action, and you should therefore focus more on what it does for your balance sheet and assets, and a little less on what it does for your income statement.

The conclusion is that a merger will succeed if (and only if) all the following are true:

- You know exactly which clients will derive benefit from the merger.
- You know exactly which benefits these are going to be.
- You have direct evidence that these clients want these benefits.
- You have a concrete action plan on exactly how you're going to achieve this extra value for clients.

If you've got all that—go ahead and merge!

16

THE ADAPTIVE FIRM

As a consultant to professional firms, I am frequently asked to speak about the future of various professions, and to forecast what the firm of the future will look like. I always refuse to do both. Predicting the future is an exercise in futility—and misses the point. The strategic challenge for professional firms is not to forecast the future, but to ensure that the firm is effective at adapting to (or otherwise responding to) already observable market changes—*whatever* they may be. Consider, for example, this list of trends in the professions:

- Fee pressure on "mature" services
- Greater mobility of partners and junior professionals
- Continued client demand for high specialization
- Increasing client demand for counseling skills and greater technical expertise
- Competition for staff from other professions/industries (change in perceived "glamour")
- Rising diversification of services inside firms—need to manage different businesses differently
- More need for investment in technology, R&D, and marketing

156

- More client demand for specific industry expertise
- Globalization of the marketplace
- Growth of microcomputer technology
- Rising and shifting training needs
- Cultural shift in work ethic among junior professionals

What is significant about this list is that it was prepared in 1982—an increasingly long time ago. Yet any listing of major trends in the professions today would probably include these same items: Even though these trends are familiar, few firms have fully responded to them. For example, just ask yourself how many firms have done the following:

- Responded to fee pressures by redesigning their methods of delivering services to achieve the same quality at lower cost
- Devised a well-functioning approach to helping their people develop counseling skills
- Effectively implemented a technology strategy that adds extra value to clients
- Created a specialization program with a high percentage of professionals committed to a specialty
- Successfully executed an effective response to global clients' need for cross-boundary coordination
- Put in place a new human-resource model to adapt to the new realities of the people marketplace

Most firms have done *something* in these areas, but few have made real progress. Certainly not as much as might be expected for a vintage 1982 trend!

Rather than being good at change, most professional firms are quite the opposite: They are resistant to it. Old ways of doing business suffer from inertia, and few firms are either willing or able to implement significant changes in the way they manage their affairs. Certainly they appear to *try:* Major trends are identified, and grand schemes are announced as responding to them—but the firmwide repair jobs tend to peter out be-

> **Rather than being good at change, most professional firms are quite the opposite: They are resistant to it.**

fore successful implementation is reached, and it's all too often back to business as usual.

In *The Devil's Dictionary,* Ambrose Bierce defines the word *plan* as "The best method of accomplishing an accidental result." There is some truth to this when it comes to professional-firm planning, most of which is a futile exercise with no observable results. However, a professional firm isn't completely at the mercy of unknowable fates and furies. You *can* make things happen if you want to, and you can be very much more or very much less prepared to face the vagaries that the unfolding future reveals. As Louis Pasteur observed, "Chance favors the prepared mind."

The trouble with most professional-firm planning is that it is full of visions, goals, missions, and ambitions—in other words, *what* we want to have happen—and completely lacking in *how* we are going to *make* it happen. One is reminded of another epigram: "The definition of an idiot is: Someone who keeps doing things the same way, and expects a different result."

Why plan in an unpredictable world? Because—through planning—you can make sure that the way you run your affairs makes you more *adaptable* and *adaptive.* Many successful firms overlook this central point. As evolutionary biologists have taught us, the more adapted (i.e., comfortable) you are in your current environment, the less likely it is that you'll be adaptive to environmental changes.

Through a combination of planning and reexamination of current management practices, firms can become better at listening to the environment and picking up its change signals early. They can also become better at ensuring that they have numerous experiments (or pilot projects) going on to test new ideas and approaches. Firms should be constantly testing what the market will and will not respond to. They must avoid complacency, and be adaptive, by constantly asking "Is there a better way to do what we do?"

Firms are very good at figuring out what they want their people to do differently. They are *not* so good at figuring out management systems to get them to do it.

Firms are very good at figuring out what they want their people to do differently. They are *not* so good at figuring out management systems to get them to do it. Inescapably, planning means *managing* in new and different ways. Many firms miss a central truth: If you haven't changed your measures and rewards, you haven't changed strategy. If you can accurately tell me what you measure and reward, I can tell you your best strategy, because I'll know what your people will go away and do in response. Accordingly, professional-firm planning must emphasize answering one question in particular: How shall we change our management practices so that our people willingly adopt new behaviors?

Such planning is not centered on a one-time, static prediction based on an impenetrable future, but rather on regularly answering the question "How do we (firm management) get better at what we do?" Well-run organizations make question-and-answer sessions of this kind a regular regimen.

If firms are to become better at responding to the environmental trends they *do* know about, a new approach is needed—one designed to focus on creating action. They should be striving to run their affairs in such a way as to become "the responsive organization," being good at designing, testing, and executing new methods of behaving so that the firm is better than the competition at adapting to new methods of doing things as market requirements shift.

This will mean creating an organization that welcomes change, rather than resisting it. For many firms, this will entail a profound shift in both firm cultures and methods of running the firm. What would characterize a responsive, adaptive, flexible organization? The firm would (at a minimum) need to be better than the competition in most of the following ways.

Aggressive Listening to the Market

A responsive firm listens continuously to its markets through every means possible, and spends less time talking at them. Good tactics include user groups, focus groups, feedback surveys, client panels, senior-partner visits, formal market research, and an organized program of attendance at client industry meetings in order to listen for new ideas, needs, and wants.

Most firms do only a little of this, and on a sporadic basis. Creating the adaptive organization requires that firms do a lot of it—routinely and systematically. When I'm invited to speak, at professional firm meetings, on "What Clients Want," my first response is always to pose the question "Have you asked your clients lately?"

Using Market Intelligence

If few firms are good at listening, fewer are good at using information gathered. The responsive firm will create numerous opportunities for groups of professionals to discuss what their clients are saying. It's not enough for planning committees and executive committees to discuss market trends and "present" the results of their deliberations. These discussions need to become the regular practice of each office, each discipline, each industry group. And these discussions must end with only one thing: a list of actions that are going to be executed.

The need to discuss market information broadly is created by the fact that professional firms are too large, too widespread, and too diverse to devise singular responses. It is not the job of top management to spot trends and devise responses, but rather to ensure (by acting as conscience and constantly asking) that each practice is actively gathering market intelligence and is devising new things to do for clients.

Raising the Level of Innovation

As too many firms have learned, aiming for grand-slam solutions leads to analysis paralysis. (How's *your* service-quality program doing?) The trick is to design an organization wherein each person and each operating group is not only encouraged, but required, to try new things. Innovation and strategy must come up from below—from the offices, the practices, the small-group teams. *They* must constantly be asked "What have you done

> **Management's job is to stimulate experiments and encourage innovation. It must create and fund lots of small-scale R&D efforts, rather than pour vast funds into grand-vision schemes.**

that's new?" and (perhaps more importantly) "What are you *going* to do that's new?" Management's job is to stimulate experiments and encourage innovation. It must create and fund lots of small-scale R&D efforts, rather than pour vast funds into grand-vision schemes.

New approaches are rarely developed through a process of debate about what the firm as a whole should do. Such large-scale change is scary. Reasons can always be found why *any* proposition is flawed, particularly if a new approach is to be adopted permanently, firmwide. The trick is not to think in terms of permanent large-scale change, but instead to talk about initial experiments or pilot programs. What can we try? Where can we test it? When and how will we know what we have learned from our experiments? How will we share the results of our learning? Only in this way can inertia be overcome, and progress be made.

Sharing New Knowledge

To be a responsive, learning organization, firms must become good at *sharing* the results of their experiments and pilot programs. There must be rewards for those who contribute to the intellectual capital of the firm by devising new methodologies, new templates and practice tools, new ideas. Most professional firms are weak at this. They do not actively work at disseminating best practice across practices and locations.

Tom Peters, in his book *Liberation Management,* describes the efforts of the consulting firm McKinsey & Co. to so capture and share its intellectual capital that what one of its professionals knows, all others have ready access to. Such knowledge-management systems are a hot topic right now, but successful implementation is still a rarity.

Contributing to the success of others should be a primary requirement of all professionals. Regretfully, it rarely is, and the firm's ability to learn is therefore compromised. An interesting illustration of this point is contained in a professional survey I frequently conduct. Among numerous questions I ask, the one that always gets the *least* agreement is *"In this firm, those who are good at business development help others to ac-quire the necessary skills.*" At most firms, helping others succeed is rarely a top priority.

Pressure for Personal Growth

If a firm is to be responsive and adaptive to its environment, then so must the people within it be. Yet many, including those who are seemingly successful, are not so inclined. It is a common observation in biology that those who are the best adapted (i.e., doing well now) are the least adaptive (i.e., able to change). Professional firms have too many people cruising—doing a good job, taking care of business, and meeting standards, but not learning and growing. Responsive firms must *demand* continuous personal growth in the individual's balance sheet (i.e., knowledge and skills). And this must be accomplished through both systems (professional-performance counseling) and personal interaction (practice leadership).

Management Behavior

A crucial role in creating the responsive organization is played out in the behavior of the practice leaders, at both firm and practice-group levels. They can either be facilitators of change, or barriers to it. All too often, managers act as brakes rather than accelerators. For understandable—if regrettable—reasons, they, more than anyone else, become focused on the short-term income statement rather than on growing the balance sheet.

Management must be perceived as leaders of a change effort, not as controllers.

Management must be perceived as leaders of a change effort, not as controllers. They need to be good at stimulating new ideas and supporting experiments, plus willing to provide seed capital for those who want to try new things. They must champion and protect those who are taking risks with innovative approaches.

Measuring Success

An adaptive firm would measure its success not only by the volume of work it performs, but also by the type of work it brings in. Are we working on new things? Do we learn from our latest projects, or are we simply milking our existing knowledge and skills? What are we doing *now* that we did not do three years ago? Such questions should be asked annually, and the answers should be used to guide new business-development efforts.

Next Steps

Try these discussion questions at one of your next small-scale meetings of professionals:

• In the past, why haven't we responded as well as we could have to environmental trends that we knew about? What has held us back? What have the barriers to change been?

• How good are we at listening to our markets in a systematic fashion? What program can we devise to ensure that our different markets tell us what they want and need? What would they like us to change?

• How can we stimulate more experimentation? How can we get more people into seeking out innovations? How can we pilot-test more new ideas?

• How can we promote the sharing of new approaches? How do we ensure that lessons learned in one place are pooled, analyzed, adapted, and disseminated? How do we ensure that what we learn is spread rapidly through the organization? How do we encourage the contribution of ideas?

• How can we encourage all firm members to strive for personal growth? How do we pay more attention to growing our assets, as well as to our short-term financials?

• What is the role of management in creating the organization that seeks out change? What should they do to *encourage* it? What do they have to do to stop *discouraging* it?

Part Three

(MOSTLY)
ABOUT YOUR CLIENTS

17

HOW REAL PROFESSIONALS DEVELOP BUSINESS

As noted in the Introduction, whenever a professional is trying to interest a client in buying an additional service, there is one thought going through the client's mind: "Why are you trying to sell me something?"

There are, of course, only two possible answers to this question. Either I believe you're really interested in me and my company, and have a sincere desire to help me, or else I believe you're just trying to generate additional revenues for your firm. Whether or not your selling effort succeeds depends solely on *which* of these two things I believe about you. If I believe you're interested in me, that you care, and that you're truly trying to help me, I'll hire you. The best way to sell is not to sell, but to *care*. Professionalism works!

The oldest saw in the professions— "Do good work and clients will come"— comes very close to the truth, as long as we recognize that the good work extends beyond technical excellence, to encom-

If your clients aren't actively telling their friends about you, maybe your work (or, of course, service) isn't as great as you think it is.

pass a true dedication to serving the clients' interests. The proof is in the pudding: If your clients aren't actively telling their friends about you, maybe your work (or, of course, service) isn't as great as you think it is. Furthermore, if you aren't getting consistently great word-of-mouth from your existing clients, you're not ready to start marketing to new ones.

If you really want to be successful in marketing your professional practice, here—in strict order—are the five things you should do. Don't move to the next thing until you've done the previous one—thoroughly and well.

First: Ask your clients how to serve them better—what they'd like you to do more of, what less of. Listen to (and do) what they say. Don't accept "You're OK." as an answer. Keep asking until they tell you how to deserve a "You're terrific!" Don't stop iterating through this until at least 90% of your clients are willing to provide you with a written testimonial, and until at least 50% of your new clients come from unsolicited referrals from your existing clients.

Second: Invest heavily in your existing clients by demonstrating an interest in their affairs. Meet with them regularly, to discuss their business; attend their internal meetings; conduct free in-house seminars for them; read their trade magazines; and do them small favors. Notice that all of this means a lot more than just entertaining and socializing with clients—that stuff is nice, but secondary. Work harder on the business relationship first, not just the personal one.

Don't stop doing this until you automatically get the overwhelming majority of their new business without even having to propose on it.

Don't invest anything *at all* in winning new clients until you're sure you've captured all the best opportunities in your existing client base!

Yes, existing clients do represent the best source of new business, but to deserve theirs, you have to earn it by being willing to invest sufficiently in the relationship. Don't invest anything *at all* in winning new clients until you're sure you've captured all the best opportunities in your existing client base! Those who have *already* retained you are owed your prior attention. *That's* professionalism.

Third: If your referrals aren't providing enough new-client business to meet your needs, go back to steps 1 and 2, and make sure you're doing all you can to follow them. Then do this: Decide which new clients you would be willing to serve *free.* You won't—but think about which ones you would serve for nothing if you *had* to.

> **Decide which new clients you would be willing to serve *free.* You won't—but think about which ones you would serve for nothing if you *had* to.**

Why this crazy thought? Simple! Clients want providers who are enthusiastic about them, interested in them, committed to them, and dedicated to them. If you're not willing to be enthusiastic, interested, committed, and dedicated, your marketing will fail. Professionals are supposed to care about their clients, aren't they? So why go after someone you don't care for? You're a professional, by George! Act like one!

If by chance you do win the business of someone you don't feel enthusiastic about, you will only have to spend your days serving someone whose business doesn't interest you. Is that what you really want? Remember that the results of your marketing will determine whatever fulfillment your career will offer—which clients you'll get to work with, what professional challenges you'll be exposed to, how much fun you'll have in your work, and so on.

Don't aim your marketing only at low-hanging fruit—dream a little. List right now who your dream clients are, and set a plan in motion to win them. If you aren't convinced yet, ask yourself what percentage of your clients you really like, and what percentage of your work you find intellectually stimulating. Are you satisfied with those percentages?

Fourth: Once you've decided whom you want to serve (and I do mean serve), design a package of activities to demonstrate—not assert—that you have a special interest in them, that you have something of value to offer them, and that you are willing to work to deserve and earn their trust.

Don't give small amounts of uncustomized attention to a lot of prospects through mailing lists, brochures, newsletters, and the like:

That's equivalent to standing on street corners saying "Do you want to do it?" You're more professional than that. Prove your interest and your worth by giving your prospects something useful: an article, a speech, a piece of research, an idea, a seminar. Prospective clients don't want unprofessional puffery. They want you to give them the evidence on which to base a sensible decision.

Fifth: Once a prospective client shows some interest in considering you, forget about talking about yourself and your firm. Successful marketing has less to do with you and your capabilities than with your abilities to find out what clients want. The key is listening, *not* talking. The key talent in good selling is being good at getting the client to tell you his or her problems, needs, wants, and concerns. Treat your prospect like a client from the minute you meet: react, give ideas, explain options, provide an education. Don't wait until you're being paid before you're helpful. You're a professional—prove it by being helpful *from the beginning.*

> **Don't wait until you're being paid before you're helpful. You're a professional—prove it by being helpful *from the beginning.***

What about all the other marketing tactics, such as brochures, newsletters, publicity, advertising? Haven't I ignored them? Yes, I certainly have, and so should you. You might want to spend some time and money in this area, but it is fatal to think that they are your primary marketing weapons. Of course it can't hurt to be quoted in the newspaper, and, yes, your client might want your brochure in his or her file to show that due diligence was done. But this is backup. All real marketing (and all real professionalism) lie in steps 1 through 5 above.

The good news is that professionalism and marketing are not in conflict with each other at all: They are the same thing. Both are defined by a dedication to being of service and helping people. As Dale Carnegie wrote in *How to Win Friends and Influence People:* You'll have more fun and success when you stop trying to get what you want, and start helping other people get what they want.

18

FINDING OUT WHAT CLIENTS WANT

The primary sources of quality failure in the professions are miscommunication and misunderstanding between the client and the professional. In turn, the largest single component of this miscommunication is over how "success" for the matter is to be defined. Professionals think they know what clients want of them, but frequently this differs from what the client truly wants (or at least expects).

An engineering client shared the following experience with me: "I had been asked by an Arab sheik to build him a bridge," he recounted. "I told him that he didn't need a bridge—and, professionally speaking, I was right. So he went to a competitor, who built him his bridge and thereby obtained for him the public glory he was looking for. In retrospect, I was completely right and completely wrong. Technically, he didn't need the bridge. But I failed to understand his *real* purposes."

Examples of this syndrome occur in every profession, on matters both small and large. (If my consulting experience is any guide, Arab sheiks are not alone in wanting showcase projects.) Phil Crosby,

171

author of *Quality Is Free,* defined quality as "conformance with customer requirements." According to this view, the first task of every professional is to uncover the client's true requirements—*whatever* they may be.

Alternate Paths to Alternate Goals

On any client project there are always a number of alternate ways of proceeding that correspond to alternate definitions of success for the assignment. First, there is the Permanent Fix—the thorough, no-holds-barred version of tackling the assignment that attempts to deal with the client problem once and for all. Understandably, but also unfortunately, this is the version that most professionals incline toward, and often *assume* that their client wants.

For example: When approached to help a firm improve its marketing success, I may be tempted to say "Ah, yes—I know what you need to do. Reorganize into industry groups, adopt a mandatory client-feedback satisfaction survey, change your compensation system, double the number of marketing-support staff to produce research-briefing booklets on each of your major clients. . . ." Even if we assume that at least some of this advice is sensible, it wouldn't be surprising if my client responded "Well, in principle that all may be correct, but I'm not in the market for so much change. How about a sales-training course for my people?"

This client is looking for a different definition of success: the Quick Impact solution. He doesn't want to go through the disruption that would be required by the Permanent Fix. He wants to hire someone to do something that will show quick results, even if these are temporary. I may want to argue, with that client, that a sales-training program will have limited impact if the incentive system is not changed to encourage partners to *use* what they've learned, and I certainly should make sure that my client understands this. But if, after this explanation is given, my client still wants to proceed with the selling-skills program, then I must accept his choice. It is useless to try to persuade the client that he *should* want the permanent fix.

There are other possible options, involving different success criteria. My client may want that version of doing the project which has the lowest up-front cost, even if it's more expensive in the long run. It is my professional responsibility to point out the costs and risks of that approach, but I can't tell my client *not* to want it. My client may want to proceed with an approach that creates the least disruption to his operations and his people, even if I think things will go better if he and his people are significantly involved at all stages.

Again, the issue is not which approach is best in a technical sense. The issue is what the client chooses *after* an informed educational discussion. As a professional, you must do three things in such a situation:

> The issue is not which approach is best in a technical sense. The issue is what the client chooses *after* an informed educational discussion.

- Identify and explain all the options available to the client.
- Help the client to understand the risks, costs, advantages, and disadvantages of each option.
- Make your professional recommendation as to which option to pursue.

If, after all of this, the client still wants to pursue a course of action that you deem unwise, then you have only two choices: Do what the client wants, or decline to be involved. But you can't (i.e., shouldn't try to) force the client to do what *you* think is right. That's not professionalism. That's arrogance.

Help Clients to Decide for Themselves

Many professionals equate their role as giving advice in the sense of recommending that the client take a particular course of action. But there are situations in which the client expects to make his or her own decision, and just wants to make sure that both sides are considering all points of view, the technical being only one of them. In this situation, the best approach is for the professional to listen as much as to speak (sometimes even avoiding the giving of advice), and to help clients to both analyze their problem and reach their own decision concerning it.

If I go to a doctor, I do *not* want him or her to say "Well—I've done my diagnosis, and you must have the leg removed as soon as possible. I've scheduled you for surgery tomorrow" What I *do* want is for the doctor to say "Well—it's serious, and I'll tell you your options. Let me make sure you understand every avenue open to you, and the risks, the costs, the advantages, and the disadvantages of each. To do my job properly, though, I must also give you my own unequivocal professional recommendation—which is that, if I were you, I'd have the leg taken off. But after all, it's *your* body, so *you* must choose."

The task of the professional is to both give the client an education in available options, and make a pertinent recommendation. It is not the task of the professional to choose.

Viewed in this way, the task of the professional is to both give the client an education in available options, and make a pertinent recommendation. It is not the task of the professional to choose. Does this mean that the professional should *always* do as the client wants? What about objectivity, independence, integrity, and professional ethics? Clearly, the client's definition of "success" or "quality" isn't always proven right, but neither is the professional's. Professional behavior is neither accepting instructions uncritically nor flat-out telling the client what to do. It must inevitably be a negotiation.

Not only is this an ethical point; it also is an approach required for sheer self-protection. If I've made sure that the client understands the limitations of the option he or she has chosen, then I have managed the expectations, and have a chance of meeting the quality standards or success measures. The key is a full and thorough mutual exploration of options—and a significant part of the professional's added value is the ability to *generate* such options.

Clearly, one cannot just say to a client, "What do you want?" The client may not know what is available to him or her. The professional must have a ready supply of "either-or's." For example, in doing retreats I frequently ask: "Do you want this meeting to cover many topics, or result in clear action plans? We can do either, but you can't have both in a limited time frame. Do you want the low-cost version, where I act as speaker but cannot comment on your firm's specific situation, or do you want to invest in getting me sufficiently educated to provide consulting advice? You can have either—but you need to weigh the pros and cons of both approaches, and give me a clear choice."

By walking my client through the options, I avoid forcing a solution. However, I try to carefully manage the client's expectations about what can and cannot be expected from the option chosen. I ensure that I am not held to a success standard that I cannot meet (for example, to develop consensus around clear action plans in a broad variety of areas, or to give customized consulting advice without investing in preparation).

Reconfirming Implicit Objectives

Those professionals who win their assignments through a proposal process may think that they can avoid this problem. Having successfully submitted a proposal and had it accepted, they are often tempted to actually begin work according to the work plan contained in the proposal. This is nearly always a mistake.

As most professionals quickly learn, the project is *never* about what they said it was during the proposal process. For example, you don't *really* find out about the client politics surrounding the project until the courtship is over. Until then, you're an outsider—denied confidential information. Only when the ring goes on the finger and you're "one of us" can you be trusted with the real truth.

> **The project is *never* about what they said it was during the proposal process. For example, you don't *really* find out about the client politics surrounding the project until the courtship is over.**

Having to deal with client politics is not an *occasional* part of professional life—it is *central* to it. Rarely does one have only a single person as the client. There always are different players with different constituencies and different objectives. Hence there is always a need to negotiate what you are taking on and what you are not, and to ensure that this is agreed to by all players. Out of sheer self-protection, it is necessary to document *which* definition of project success you are following.

As soon as you have a signed contract, your first task is to go back to the client and confirm (or reconfirm) what he or she *really* expects of you, and how the matter is to be conducted. Assuming that all relevant details are covered in your initial understanding can prove fatal. Many seemingly low-level, but indeed crucial, details usually are left undiscussed before the matter is awarded. With whom, exactly, will you need to consult in the client organization during the conduct of the matter? Precisely what form and frequency of communication does the client really want? Exactly what will you need from the client in the form of information and participation? Do all relevant client personnel understand and agree with the objectives outlined initially, or are there still internal conflicts to be resolved? All this, and more, needs to be discussed and—preferably—documented.

Many professionals avoid such "clarification" meetings early in the relationship (i.e., as soon as the deal is won), not wanting to dull the glamour of the courtship by discussing mundane matters. However, the longer it is postponed, the longer ambiguity will exist about what the client is *really* looking for, and this ambiguity will lead either to perceptions of poor quality ("You're not doing what I expected") or to economic problems ("I'm not paying for that; it's not in the scope of what we agreed to"). The perfect time to renegotiate the "psychological" contract, or even the financial one, is as soon as you know about, or can uncover, a change in client expectations.

Changes in Scope Always Happen

If it is a mistake to assume that you know what the client wants at the start of the assignment, it is disastrous to assume that the client's goals will remain unchanged. What initially appeared to them as an aspirin matter may clearly become one requiring major surgery as your work proceeds. As many professionals tell me, changes in scope are among their biggest problems. But there is no need for problems here: All that is required is a well-documented, *precise* memo of understanding at the beginning, and an ongoing series of quality-negotiation conversations aimed at answering such questions as "Are we still on track? Do you still want the Quick Fix version on which we agreed? Is the level of communication adequate?"

As should be clear, the purpose of these conversations is not only to get feedback and monitor your quality, but perhaps more importantly to ensure that the client's goals and success criteria haven't changed. Quality must be negotiated—continually.

Is Everyone On Board?

One final point should be made—and it is crucial. Not only must the professional and all relevant client personnel share a common understanding of the goals for the assignment, but all those working on the matter must understand which version of success they are aiming to achieve—*this* time.

Unless specifically instructed otherwise, junior members of the team will do their part of the work in the way they (successfully) did it last time, assuming that that's how things are *supposed* to be done. Too many lead professionals delegate work without giving clear instructions on scope, format, time budget, *real* deadlines, and the relative priorities among different subtasks. It is not surprising, therefore, that they get back a work product that causes them to say "That's not what I wanted!" If miscommunications within the client are the leading source of quality problems, miscommunications within the project team are a close second, and the cause of the problem is identical: poor communication about what a quality job is going to mean *this time*.

> **Too many lead professionals delegate work without giving clear instructions on scope, format, time budget, *real* deadlines, and the relative priorities among different subtasks.**

19

WHY CROSS-SELLING HASN'T WORKED

Every professional service firm I have ever encountered has had, and still has, the goal of cross-selling—expanding relationships with existing clients in order to increase the range of services delivered. Yet success in this area has been limited. Few firms, if any, have made cross-selling work on a systematic basis. And there is a simple explanation for this apparent failure: Firms have been going about it in the wrong way.

Who Benefits?

Firms have traditionally exhorted their professionals to tell the client about "the other things we do," but have become frustrated when this produces minimal results. In consequence, they have come to view the barriers to making cross-selling happen as primarily internal: a lack of trust across departments; professionals being protective of their individual client relationships; or incentive systems that cause professionals to worry more about the revenues of their own department than about helping other departments in the firm. These internal barriers are real, and deadly. But there is an even more powerful reason why cross-selling efforts have historically failed: Cross-selling does little, if anything, for the *client*.

It is obvious what cross-selling will do for the firm: increase revenues, and cement client relationships. These are valid and powerful reasons to emphasize this area. But the fact that something is good for the firm is an insufficient test. In any business there is an iron-clad rule which says that if what you are planning to do truly adds value for the clients, you can then benefit from creating that additional value. If it doesn't do anything extra for the clients and just benefits you, then it is almost certainly unsustainable, and will fail.

> If what you are planning to do truly adds value for the clients, you can then benefit from creating that additional value. If it doesn't do anything extra for the clients and just benefits you, then it is almost certainly unsustainable, and will fail.

What does cross-selling do for the client? Usually nothing. In the traditional approach to cross-selling, firms supplying one service attempt to get their clients to use the firms for a (distinct) second service, to be performed by a totally distinct group of professionals within the firm. But what does the client get from this that couldn't obtained by going through a sensible selection process for that second service, independent of the first? If there is little or no overlap in the staffing of the project, why should the client care that the professionals on the second project are in the same firm as the first?

To say that the client benefits because we have terrific skills in the second service area is beside the point. If they're so terrific, your group in that additional area will win the business on their own merits when the client searches for the best firm to handle their need. What is needed is a reason that shows the client that there will be extra benefit from using multiple departments of the *same* firm, above and beyond the individual excellence of each department.

What might this extra benefit be? There are real possibilities, the most obvious of which is this: If the first team serving the client has developed a significant understanding of the client's business, and can share that experience in such a way that it makes the second team more efficient or effective, then the client can *clearly* benefit. Note that to pull this off requires teaming across internal firm boundaries. It requires the original professional serving the client to be actively involved helping the new team in such a way that it benefits the client.

What, therefore, should be pursued is not an engagement for some other professional to work on independently, but some form of joint project. Firms should not be asking their people to sell their partners, but to look for ways for partners in different disciplines to work together. There is thus a critical distinction between traditional cross-selling (where there is no overlap in the delivery of the two distinct services) and integrated selling (of joint, multidisciplinary services), where the client has a chance to receive extra value. "Pure" cross-selling is hard to justify, but integrated services have a fair shot at working.

> **There is thus a critical distinction between traditional cross-selling (where there is no overlap in the delivery of the two distinct services) and integrated selling (of joint, multidisciplinary services), where the client has a chance to receive extra value. "Pure" cross-selling is hard to justify, but integrated services have a fair shot at working.**

It is worth observing that not only does integrated selling do something for the client, but also it helps overcome some of the internal barriers referred to above. If I am asked to sell the services of some other professional on a matter on which I will not be involved, I am subject to all the trust and incentive issues that professionals traditionally worry about. However, if I am looking for follow-on work which will require both the services of another professional *and* my services, then I have less risk and more direct incentive.

Why Are You Here?

Even if we assume that the firm has figured out a way to make combined—not just additional—services of value to the client, there still remain some barriers to winning client acceptance. Firms must get *organized* in order to market to existing clients. Many firms have appropriately appointed client-relationship partners to oversee the firm's dealing with key accounts. Further, they have correctly assigned specific individuals from other disciplines to be members of the team created to market to these specific individual clients. These teams develop *client-service plans* meant to foster the relationship with the target client. However, problems still remain. Too many client-service plans are not really about giving service at all—they're sales plans. Part of the problem is in the very phrase itself, cross-*selling*.

What many professionals fail to realize about selling to existing clients is that clients expect us to *earn* their follow-on business. For example, how many professionals volunteer to attend (at no charge) internal client-management meetings to act as a resource? Or offer to critique, at no charge, a client's internal study, as a gesture of good faith? And how many demonstrate a willingness to earn the next piece of work and not take it for granted? The answer to all of these questions is *very few*.

Unfortunately, the average professional doesn't demonstrate much interest in the client's business. As a litmus test, I frequently take a poll of professionals in order to ask how many regularly read the trade magazines of their top one or two clients. It is the rare firm wherein the proportion of professionals that do this exceeds 10%. It is hard to convince a client that you care about his or her business when it is evident that you don't know what's going on in it.

> It is hard to convince a client that you care about his or her business when it is evident that you don't know what's going on in it.

A truly effective client-service plan will include a set of activities that will help professionals to get to know the client's business better and in a more organized way. (It should be noted that this is not something that can be done only by partners. Smart firms make good use of junior professionals, marketing-support staffs, and significant others, to ensure that partners have the latest business intelligence on their clients.) A good client-service plan will also include activities meant to deepen the business relationship by expanding the amount of client contact, both on and off the current assignment.

As an example of a creative approach to knowing the client's business better, consider the practice of a certain major consulting firm. Every two weeks, all those working on an individual client project get together to discuss what each team member (from the most senior partner to the most junior associate) has learned about what is going on in the client's business since last they met—*two weeks before*! New entrants quickly learn that, when assigned to a client project, they have two responsibilities: to execute their technical tasks, and to learn as much as possible about the client organization. Even the most junior member of the professional staff quickly learns that he or she should be establishing relationships with counterparts in the client organization, and expressing an interest in the client's business. Not surprisingly, this firm has an outstanding track record of expanding its client relationships. As a not-so-coincidental side benefit, this attention is usually received by the client not as oppressive, but as a welcome, flattering interest in the business.

Unfortunately, examples such as this are all too rare. Too many professionals demonstrate *no* interest in the client, beyond the details of the current matter. They've never discussed the client's strategic plan, they've never sat in on a client's internal meeting, they don't read the client's trade rags—and then they expect the client to give them more business!

What Clients Want

Clients tell me that they not only welcome their providers' bringing new ideas—they *expect* that. They do want their outside advisors to keep them apprised of things that they should consider, but what they don't want is a hard sell on every one.

The paradox is that clients *do* want their firms to market to them. In the numerous client panels I have moderated for firms in different professions, I always ask clients how they feel about their outside providers' giving them suggestions for new assignments. The answers are almost uniform: Clients tell me that they not only welcome their providers' bringing new ideas—they *expect* that. They do want their outside advisors to keep them apprised of things that they should consider, but what they don't want is a hard sell on every one. "If there are additional things your firm can help my company with, of course I want to hear about it," one client said, "We have a mutual interest in doing anything that helps my company. So keep those ideas coming. Just don't expect me to buy every time. Service me, don't sell me!"

Making It Happen

There's good news in all of this. Cross-selling *can* be made to work. But firms must recognize that cross-selling is like a Ph.D. program: There are milestones that must be passed before you are eligible even to try it.

First comes the Bachelor's Degree program of conducting the current assignment in such a way that the client is not only satisfied but delighted. The client needs to be left thinking "Not only did they get me a good result, but it was a pleasure to work with them." It should be obvious that there's no point in trying to generate more work from existing clients unless you have left them eager to work with you again. This is the familiar "client service and satisfaction program" that has been much discussed in recent years.

Next comes the Master's Degree program of investing in the client relationship so that the firm is visibly seen by the client as trying to earn and deserve future work. The emphasis here needs to be on investing, *not* on selling. For example, are we putting on free inside seminars for the client's personnel? Are we performing special studies at our own expense in order to bring to the client information that is customized to the situation at hand?

If we have delighted the client on the current matter, and clearly been seen to be willing to invest in the relationship, then (and only then) can we show up and say, for example, "Our knowledge of your situation suggests that you really ought to look at X. May we bring our specialist partner in to talk to you about this?" Unfortunately, firms historically have neglected delighting or superpleasing the client, and instead have omitted investing in the relationship, just showing up and asking "Do you want to buy something else?" Of course, the only possible answer is "No, thanks." Too many cross-selling programs start with what we've got, and try to push that onto the client.

To be effective, cross-selling must begin with a deep understanding of the client's business, including an educated, up-to-date knowledge about what sort of sticky problems or issues the client faces. And a little bit of sincerity, based on a true desire to help, wouldn't hurt the cause one bit.

20

MEASURING YOUR MARKETING SUCCESS

When I ask those who work in professional service firms what formal measures they use to monitor the success of their marketing efforts, the most common response is "Well, if revenues go up, we feel we've succeeded." Similarly, when I have sat in on practice-group marketing meetings, it is invariably gross revenues that they discuss. This all seems reasonable—but, as we shall see, revenues are an insufficient (and potentially misleading) indicator of marketing success.

What the revenue measure fails to reflect is that marketing in a professional firm is (or should be) about getting *better* business, not just *more* business. Firms should spend more time tracking and formally monitoring the caliber of business they bring in, and not just its volume. Yet few firms have such mechanisms in place.

> Revenues are an insufficient (and potentially misleading) indicator of marketing success.
>
> Marketing in a professional firm is (or should be) about getting *better* business, not just *more* business.

What do I mean by "better" business? There are two tests that new

185

business must meet in order to be classified as better business: the income-statement test and the balance-sheet test.

The Income-Statement Test

The income-statement test is simplicity itself: Work is better business if it is more profitable than work that the firm traditionally obtains. This should seem so obvious as to not merit much discussion. In principle, most firms would claim that they take profitability considerations into account when deciding where to place their marketing efforts. The reality, however, often is different. I have observed more than a few firms whose approach to practice development is "If it moves, shoot it." Or, to phrase it another way, "We've never seen a piece of new business we didn't like."

Profitability considerations, in practice, often end up being ignored in marketing. Individuals pursue every opportunity presented to them, and a few that aren't. Above all else, generating *volume* is the underlying marketing philosophy. Yet there are many firms who were so successful in their marketing that they ended up with lower profits per partner than when they started. Taking in every piece of low-profit business you can get is a fine way to grow, but I wouldn't call it great marketing.

Firms do this for a number of reasons, one being insecurity. If you are not confident about your ability to attract and win the best business, then it's easy to justify that you have to go after any business you can. Of course, this can be (and *is,* in many firms I have observed) a self-fulfilling prophecy. Practice groups get so busy proposing on every request for proposal they see that they have no *time* to go after better business. If it is suggested that they should propose on fewer low-profit, low-probability opportunities and spend the extra time more productively on some other part of the marketing effort, one gets the reaction "We couldn't do that! You mean actually decline to respond to a proposal opportunity? We *never* do that!"

A second cause of this behavior is that firms tend to overemphasize "business origination" (i.e., marketing success) in their performance criteria for senior professionals. The more business you generate, the better you look. Rarely do firms have systems in place equipped or inclined to ask "Was the business that this person generated profitable?" When performing statistical analyses on compensation systems, I almost always discover that, although there usually is a correlation between the volume of revenues generated and compensation, there either is no measure of engagement profitability, or else it exists but is not correlated with compensation awards. Quite simply, the firm's professionals believe that they'll be rewarded for bringing in business—period. Profitability is nice, but secondary.

The firm's professionals believe that they'll be rewarded for bringing in business—period. Profitability is nice, but secondary.

In many firms, this isn't an unintended side-effect—they truly do believe that all new business is good business (especially in a recession). They argue that they must keep their people busy, and that even less-than-fully-profitable work is economical if their staff would otherwise be idle. This argument is an irrefutable example of short-term thinking. *Of course* low-profit work is better than no work—*this* year. But again, this can hardly be called marketing success: Taking any work you can get is no way to build a business. To be successful, a firm must win more than its fair share of the profitable work, and marketing-success measures must be established to track this.

There is an additional problem here. Many firms that do measure profitability at the engagement or project level use proxy measures for profitability, such as *realization rate* (the percentage of standard fees that the project will command). But this is an insufficient measure. Profits do indeed come from high fees and high margins, but firm owners or partners can also make high profits by taking in lower-fee work which allows good leverage (i.e., a high ratio of employees to owners or partners). To properly track their marketing success, firms need to have a costing system which reveals the true (fully costed) profitability of each job. Only then can they tell whether their marketing efforts are helping them to improve. (See Chapter 13 for related information.)

The Balance-Sheet Test

If we're bringing in profitable work, then our marketing must be working—yes? Unfortunately—no! There's another hurdle to jump over. We must ask ourselves whether or not we are bringing in work that will help us to improve our skills and stay competitive. The jobs that professionals work on can be either asset-*milking* (taking advantage of and exploiting existing skills, relationships, and reputation) or asset-*building* (offering the opportunity to develop new skills by working on frontier innovative projects, building new and stronger client relationships that will pay dividends in future years, and creating a reputation in new fields or market segments).

But too much asset-milking work will leave the firm exposed strategically. Skills and reputations depreciate over time, and only by building new skills, relationships, and reputations can a firm thrive over time.

Which of the two types of work is generated by a firm's marketing efforts is critical to its success. In any given year, either asset-milking *or* asset-building work can generate good current profits. But too much asset-milking work will leave the firm exposed strategically. Skills and reputations depreciate over time, and only by building new skills, relationships, and reputations can a firm thrive over time.

Most firms would agree with this reasoning, and even accept it intellectually. However, it is the rare firm that has found a way to build this reasoning into its management practices. How many firms have a functioning formal screen set up to evaluate new business opportunities based upon their asset value? How many firms regularly review their mix of new business, and assess not only the quantity of the practice but also its caliber? The answer is: relatively few.

Doing these things is not complicated. Here's one effective way to build it into your management process: Every three months or so, each of your practice groups (discipline groups, offices, industry teams, etc.) should get together and pull out a list of every new engagement they have worked on in the previous quarter. Someone from outside the practice group (a managing partner, or a group

FIGURE 20.1

Assessing the Caliber of the Practice

Did this assignment:
- Allow us to learn new skills?
- Expose us to an *important* new client (prominence, source of referrals, etc.)?
- Increase (not just sustain) an important existing client relationship?
- Allow us to leverage more than in the past?
- Allow us to command higher fees than in the past?
- Allow us to work "higher" in the client organization?
- Introduce us to a new industry?
- Lead to other work with this client?

---

head from a different group) should attend, to play the role of friendly skeptic.

At the meeting, each new engagement is assigned a set of scores, using the criteria shown in the Figure 20.1. In essence, you will be probing to ask "What did this piece of business do for us?" The answer "It provided revenue and kept us busy" is nice enough, but should never be accepted as sufficient. There truly is good revenue and less-good revenue, and firms must be honest with themselves about which they have.

Naturally, no firm will want to be idealistic concerning this review; not all engagements provide skill-building opportunities. (After all, the baby *does* have to be fed.) However, if a majority of the assignments fall at the low end, it will be obvious that, whatever the revenue growth has been, there still is marketing to be done.

Specific guidance on marketing will also be generated quarter-by-quarter. Perhaps in one period you are doing well on generating important new clients, but have done nothing to deepen your relationships with important key accounts. This review will highlight that, and suggest where your marketing efforts next period need to be placed.

The presence of a "third party" friendly skeptic is important in making this review process a practical management tool. If the team

If the team is asked to rate itself, it is very easy to rationalize any piece of new business. is asked to rate itself, it is very easy to rationalize any piece of new business. A case can always be made that a given new client is "important," and that a new project "offers us the opportunity to learn something new." It is healthy to have someone play the "challenging" role to expose these rationalizations.

It should be stressed that this qualitative review of the caliber of the practice does *not* imply more meetings associated with running the practice. Most firms already get together regularly to discuss marketing efforts and results. All that is being proposed is that the group begin with its traditional discussions, and then add this balance-sheet review as a regular part of all marketing meetings.

After some practice with this system, the questions asked here can be used not just as a look-back device; they can also become part of a *prospective* screening process set up to determine where marketing efforts should go, and which opportunities are (or are not), worth pursuing. My strong advice is to begin with the regular look-back process, which is easier to enforce. Experience has shown that in all but the smallest of firms, effective prospect screening is a difficult process to administer, indeed.

Marketing Statistics

An additional way to monitor and track the caliber of your practice is to pay attention to certain key marketing ratios. Consider the following examples, each of which is introduced by a pertinent question.

What percentage of your revenues will recur next year without any effort? Naturally, some professions (say audit or actuarial) have an easier time estimating this than others, but the exercise is a useful one for *every* professional firm. Go down the list of your existing clients, and estimate how much revenue that client is going to provide you next year.

Yes, it will be an estimate, but forcing your lead professionals on each account to answer this question will inveigle them into productive reflections on the strength of the relationship, where the client's business is going, and (not coincidentally) what you and your firm have to do to ensure that continued revenue stream.

What is your total marketing capacity, measured in person-hours? This simple question, unanswered in many firms, requires only that each person involved in business development either declares or is assigned a fixed (or at least a minimum) amount of nonbillable time that he or she has agreed to contribute to the marketing effort.

Many firms can readily tell you their marketing expenditures (after all, *that's cash!*) but not the hours spent thereon. Yet it is the hours invested, and not the cash spent, that is determinative of marketing success. If you don't know your aggregate marketing-hours capacity, how can you manage your marketing efforts? And if you can't manage your marketing efforts, how can you hope for marketing success?

How many person-hours do you spend on a typical proposal? I am always surprised at how few firms have a ready answer to this question. Only *some* firms—the exceptions—can tell you precisely the time, as well as cost, of each and every professional and support person invested in pursuing each specific opportunity as relentlessly as necessary.

The reasons for keeping track of this are obvious: It is exceedingly helpful to know how much it costs you to acquire each piece of business, so that you can both track your return on selling investment and continue to learn about where to place your marketing resources. Obvious—but not always observed.

What percentage of assignments that you pursue do you win? Again, I am amazed at how many firms can answer only with impressionistic guesses. In the *best* firms, a detailed analysis of these statistics shows not only the number of assignments won and lost, but also patterns in which kinds of jobs the firm tends to win.

For example, what is the average monetary size of the proposals you win, versus the average size of the ones you lose? Do you tend to win the bigger ones or the smaller ones, or is there no difference? Do you tend to win more with bigger clients than with smaller ones? Are there industry trends in which jobs you win or lose? Questions such as these will tell you as much about your market image and your market's perception of you as will any market-research study.

What is the size of your average assignment? Since small jobs often take as much marketing effort as large ones, there are obvious economies of scale in marketing. For most professional firms, it will also tend to be true that, on average, your larger jobs will be more profitable. Hence "average size of job" is a key measure of marketing success.

Naturally, one must avoid fooling oneself here. If your work tends to be divided into phases, then care must be exercised in defining this measure. Some firms finesse the issue by examining total revenue per client, rather than per assignment. While this is sometimes necessary, it is unfortunate because it says very different things about your marketing if you have lots of small jobs for a client, or a lesser number of larger jobs. Hence it is worth trying to calculate (and pay attention to) average job size.

What percentage of all fees spent by clients on services in your area do they pay to you? Total revenues per client is an interesting statistic. But far more interesting is the percentage penetration. Are you one of a number of vendors to them, or are you their dominant (or at least preferred) supplier? Quantifying this can of course be tricky, since you need to ask the clients how much they might spend—but you would be surprised how many clients will cooperate by giving you a ballpark figure.

Even if you have to estimate heroically, it's worth asking yourself how many of your clients demonstrate by their actions that they view you as their dominant or lead supplier. Client relationships that will predictably and reliably produce future revenue should be treated as being among your most valued assets—and you ought to keep close tabs on your assets. Don't finish reviewing your marketing efforts until you've got a good handle on this one!

What percentage of your business is won on a noncompetitive, sole-source basis? (This interesting marketing statistic is related to the first statistic discussed above.) This ratio is probably the best measure of quality that you have. If the percentage is low, it means that you don't have a market niche that thinks of you as either differentiated or the quality leader in your practice area. Or, stated another way: The quality of your referrals is not good enough. Note that there's a world of difference between referrals such as "Yes, they are competent; you should consider them" and those that say "They are the only people to use!"

What percentage of this year's revenues are from clients you had never worked for prior to this year? (This is the obverse of the repeat-business ratio, the percentage of revenues from existing clients.) Let this new-client ratio get too high, and you'll find yourself working harder at marketing than is necessary.

What percentage of your top 10 clients were top 10 clients three or five years ago? This is yet one more way to examine your client-retention rate (and hence your need for new-client marketing). The topic is sufficiently important to examine in multiple ways.

What percentage of your revenues come from services you didn't offer three or five years ago? This new-service ratio is becoming increasingly important as the professions continue to experience rapidly changing client needs.

I am sure there are other ratios used to monitor marketing efforts that would shed light on the caliber of your practice. Figure one out that would help you to learn something about your practice! Meanwhile, check out the summary list shown in Figure 20.2: How many of the questions can you answer about *your* practice?

Summary

In discussing these concepts with professional firms around the world, I frequently hear the following objection: "David, aren't you being unrealistic? After all, times are tough and we have to be grateful for *any* business we can get. Yet you're telling us to worry about the "asset value" of our work. Isn't this an unreasonable standard?"

My answer is "No." While readily acknowledging that in tough times a firm may need to accept work that scores low on the criteria in my questionnaire, it is nevertheless a reality of professional life that the firm's future depends on bringing in asset-building work.

If a firm is not building new skills, strengthening existing relation-

FIGURE 20.2

Which of These Marketing Statistics Do You Monitor?

Recurring-Business Ratio: *What percentage of your revenues will recur next year without any effort?*

Capacity: *What is your total marketing capacity, measured in person-hours?*

Proposal Budget: *How many person-hours do you spend on a typical proposal?*

Win–Loss Ratio: *What percentage of assignments that you pursue do you win?*

Assignment Size: *What is the size of your average assignment?*

Penetration Ratio: *What percentage of all fees spent by clients on services in your area do they pay to you?*

Sole-Source Ratio: *What percentage of your business is won on a noncompetitive, sole-source basis?*

New-Client Ratio: *What percentage of this year's revenues are from clients you had never worked for prior to this year?*

Client-Retention Ratio: *What percentage of your top 10 clients were top 10 clients three or five years ago?*

New-Service Ratio: *What percentage of your revenues come from services you didn't offer three or five years ago?*

---

ships, and creating new ones, then its future is truly at risk. And the responsibility for ensuring that future lies with the wise management of marketing efforts, incorporating balance-sheet thinking into the basic-volume orientation that most marketing efforts are built on today. Yes, marketing is even more complicated—and important— than you thought it was.

21

SATISFACTION GUARANTEED

Christopher Hart has written a fascinating and important book, *Extraordinary Guarantees* (New York: AMACOM, 1993), which shows how service firms can gain a competitive advantage by explicitly guaranteeing their work. Consider the guarantee given by Hart's own consulting firm specializing in quality issues:

"Our work is guaranteed to the complete satisfaction of the client. If the client is not completely satisfied with our services, we will, at the client's option, either waive professional fees, or accept a portion of those fees that reflects the client's level of satisfaction."

At first this might look outrageous and extreme: A professional firm guaranteeing its work? Surely the work of a consulting firm (or law, accounting, or any other professional firm) is subject to so many contingencies that *nothing* can be guaranteed. Isn't Hart's firm taking an extraordinary amount of risk?

Think a little more, and the idea doesn't (or shouldn't) sound outrageous at all. Notice that Hart's firm doesn't guarantee a specific result (which *would* be impossible, as well as contrary to many professional

195

codes of ethics)—rather, it guarantees the client's complete satisfaction—to which most firms *say* they are dedicated anyway.

> **The professional-firm marketplace is cluttered with claims to excellence and assertions of quality, few of which are credible to the buyer for the simple reason that that's *all* they are— claims and assertions.**

The professional-firm marketplace is cluttered with claims to excellence and assertions of quality, few of which are credible to the buyer for the simple reason that that's *all* they are—claims and assertions. A firm that has the courage to offer an unconditional guarantee will break through this clutter by saying to the market "Don't take our word for it. Decide for yourself."

Consider the alternative. Without a guarantee, what is a firm saying to its clients? "We're committed to your complete satisfaction, but if we fail to please you, we expect to be paid anyway!" Leaving all considerations of ethics aside, this is just bad business—and it isn't how the real world works. The reality of today's marketplace is that if your client is unsatisfied, you're probably going to have to adjust the fee, like it or not. But that shouldn't either surprise or terribly upset you, because your professionals have long since sat down with the timesheets, looked at the work done, compared it to what was projected, and made judgments on what could realistically be collected as well as billed. The guiding principle is, or should be, what Gerald Weinberg advised in his book *Secrets of Consulting* (New York: Dorset House, 1985): "If they don't like your work, don't take their money."

If anyone thinks that this approach is theoretical, futuristic, or infeasible, he or she should consider the fact that a number of American corporations (e.g., General Electric) are now purchasing their legal services on the proviso of using a hold-back system. In this approach, the law firm bills the corporation the normal hourly billing rate system, but the corporation pays only 80% (or some such percentage) of each invoice, putting the remaining 20% into escrow. At the end of the year, the corporation reviews its satisfaction with all that the law firm has done for it, and then decides, at its sole discretion, how much of the remaining 20% to pay out.

What is this system if not a form of satisfaction guarantee? The difference between what GE is doing and what **"If they don't like your work, don't take their money."** Hart advocates is that GE is *imposing* this system upon its outside vendors, and Hart advocates that firms take the initiative and *propose* such billing systems, differentiating themselves from their competition by their unconditional willingness to stand behind their work.

If bills related to client satisfaction are increasingly a reality, why not make a virtue of necessity? I can report that the benefits are real: I have actuarial, consulting, legal, and engineering clients, all of whom have won business they might not otherwise have obtained without the use of guarantees.

Who Decides Value?

Both the hold-back and guarantee billing systems are reflections of the new value-billing environment in which it is the client, not the provider, who determines what value has been received. There are other variants of the same principle. Consider, for example, a practice I call *performance billing.*

Suppose that a firm is bidding for work, but is told that, while it is the leading contender, its fees are too high. What options does it have? Of course, one is caving in up-front and cutting fees. Another is trying to stick with the firm's original fee level and be persuasive on why you're worth what you propose to charge. *Neither* of these two extremes is likely to lead to a satisfactory result.

Instead, consider an offer along these grounds: "Dear Client: We understand that you have no basis to be able to judge up-front, before we do the project, that we are worth the fees we charge. We can't ask you to blindly place your trust in our claims. However, we do really believe that we can render full value for our fees. So, we propose the following. During the project, we'll bill you 75% of our normal fees. At the conclusion of the project, when the evidence is in, you (and you alone) will decide what our work was worth and you, and you alone, will decide your level of satisfaction and pay us a (final) balloon payment. Since we are taking the risk on the downside, and since you will get to determine the size of the end payment, can we agree that the range for the total payment will be between 75% and 125% of our initial fee request?"

This approach is nothing more than betting on one's own professionalism, and on one's related ability to satisfy the client. This approach is nothing more than betting on one's own professionalism, and on one's related ability to satisfy the client. Having experimented with it myself, I can report that it has helped me to get hired where otherwise I would not have been; and I am also happy to report that (so far) I have never been ripped off—I have never received less than my regular fees, and sometimes have received more. Do I expect to get ripped off sometime? Yes, I do. Do I think that the extra business won by this pricing approach will more than compensate me for those rare instances? Absolutely!

It is also relevant to note that I (like everyone else) have been on the other side of this issue, as a buyer of services. A while ago I had some wooden cabinets made by a skilled craftsman. His price was high, and I had a dilemma. I wanted a fine work product, but I also wanted it quickly, and I wanted it made and installed at my convenience. I wanted to create an incentive for this artisan, but I couldn't specify precisely what I wanted. If I created an incentive for quick delivery, I would run the risk of shoddy work. If I wanted the ability to make changes in the specifications midstream (and I did), then I would run the risk of late delivery.

How could I create an alignment of incentives? An hourly basis wouldn't give me comfort, and a fixed fee would provide no incentive. The answer was as given above: I told this person that I would pay his bid price, but that I would be willing to pay up to 10% more at the end of the project if I was happy. "Happy" was, by design, ill-defined. There was not a finite list of objective criteria, no concrete goals.

The result was as desired. Not only did I get a magnificent cabinet, but I was kept informed, consulted, and made comfortable by a high level of attentive service. The extra 10% proved a bargain: It reduced my risk, it allayed my concerns about what he was doing, and it kept me from sleepless nights. I didn't have to watch over this contractor like a hawk, worrying that he would be trying to shave a little here and there. I had made it worth his while to please me.

These experiences reveal an important lesson about clients' attitudes toward fees. What is frequently overlooked is that, apart from the issue of the amount of cash that will have to be paid out, clients are also troubled by issues of uncertainty, ambiguity, control, and risk. When clients agree to a traditional (hourly billing) form of payment, they effectively must hand over to you the management of their money. They may be more than willing to pay high fees for things they really need—but, by agreeing to pay you on an hourly basis for everything you do, they must *trust* that you will be efficient, that you will manage things well, and that you will not spend their money on unnecessary activities.

> Apart from the issue of the amount of cash that will have to be paid out, clients are also troubled by issues of uncertainty, ambiguity, control, and risk.

As is only too clear, clients do not accept on faith that their outside provider always does these things well. Quite the opposite: They clearly believe (with justification) that, unless closely watched, their outside firm will be inefficient, and their project poorly managed. It is for this reason that we are beginning to see such prevalent client demands for budgets, estimates, and detailed time- and progress-reporting. These devices are as much about getting control over professional service bills as they are about reducing them.

As my story about the cabinetmaker attempts to show, many clients would be willing to pay *more* than normal if they could be confident that their interests were more perfectly aligned with the outside provider's. Which, of course, brings us back to Hart's guarantee system. What better system for aligning interests and sharing risks than a system that says "Pay me if you're happy"?

Making the Guarantee Work

How does a professional (or a professional firm) get started with a guarantee? Hart, appropriately, counsels caution. He suggests piloting the guarantee in a small number of assignments with a carefully selected group of clients. The case could be made that the guarantee is most powerful with *new* clients, and of more value to the firm in the sense of bringing in work it might not otherwise have won. It remains sensible, however, to test the system with *existing* clients. Obviously it is not feasible to guarantee, for the same client, one matter and not another. Once the guarantee is offered, it must be offered on *all* matters for the client.

Caution is also required in figuring out which client executive gets to determine value. Who, precisely, is the client officer who will make the satisfaction judgment? I can clearly bring to mind situations where the decision-making process was so confused that I would not be comfortable giving a guarantee to satisfy everyone involved. However, this might be as much an indication of a type of work I should not take on as it is an indicator of how to price the work.

A guarantee would also force firms to think carefully about which clients it wanted to work for.

A guarantee would also force firms to think carefully about which clients it wanted to work for. If I am required to trust my client to pay me fairly, then I must extend my guarantees only to clients with whom I feel comfortable. This is not an approach which will maximize volume, but rather one which maximizes reputation and true relationship-building. Not a bad result!

Finally, firms interested in the client-decides-value concept must decide whether to offer this form of pricing on a project-by-project basis, or (as in the GE situation) based on the totality of work done for that client.

These concerns aside, it is relatively clear what a firm must do to be successful with client-decides-value pricing. It needs to ensure that, at the beginning of every assignment, there is a clear, mutually shared understanding of the client's needs, what the project will aim to accomplish, and how that goal will be achieved (see Chapter 18). This is no more than what should happen anyway in any halfway decent client relationship, but all too often doesn't.

Beyond agreement on goals, a reliance on client satisfaction to determine fees would *commit* the firm (and of course the individuals within it) to perform those elements of client service that all firms *talk* about but few *execute:* getting to know the client's business; keeping the client informed about project status; involving the client at appropriate points in the assignment, to ensure client approval, and so on. This is nothing more than a level of client communications that clients *already* require.

The new pricing approach would also require that the lead professional act as an effective project manager, ensuring that all members of the engagement team know what is required of them, know what is important, and are working effectively together. This is nothing more than what all clients *already* expect.

All this proves a trivial but powerful conclusion: If you're already good at these activities (being close to clients in relationships marked by mutual trust, negotiating clear goals, having good client communications, performing effective project-team management), you'll have little risk in offering a guarantee—and you can capitalize on your superior quality. If you're *not* already good at these things, and see a guarantee as putting a lot of cash at risk—well, maybe you're not as good as you think you are.

A guarantee *forces* a firm to live up to its own quality claims. As Hart points out, the power of a guarantee may lie less in the marketing benefit than in the discipline it imposes to (at last) deliver on the quality rhetoric. If you're *really* aiming to be the quality leader in your market, why not put your money where your mouth is?

One final point, in case you're wondering: Yes, I always guarantee—unconditionally—client satisfaction in my consulting work!

In case you're wondering: Yes, I always guarantee—unconditionally—client satisfaction in my consulting work!

INDEX

Continued from page iv
"No Regrets" (as "Go for What You [Really] Want," in *Legal Business,* January/February 1996); "It's About Time" (in *Legal Business,* May 1996); "Are You Willing to Be Managed?" (in *Legal Business,* April 1996); "Why Should I Follow You?" (in *Legal Business,* December 1995); "Values in Action" (in *Legal Business,* September 1995); "The Value of Intolerance" (in *The American Lawyer,* September 1994); "A Time for Healing" (in *The American Lawyer,* June 1993); "How Firms (Should) Add Value" (in *The American Lawyer,* December 1993); "Success Through Skill-Building" (in *The American Lawyer,* November 1993); "What Kind of Provider Are You?" (two parts, in *Legal Business,* October 1996 and November 1996); "Managing Your Client's Projects" (as "Measuring Engagement Profitability," in *The American Lawyer,* July/August 1994); "Why Merge?" (in *Legal Business,* March 1996); "The Adaptive Firm" (in *The American Lawyer,* June 1993); "How Real Professionals Develop Business" (in *Accountancy,* September 1994); "Finding Out What Clients Want" (in *The American Lawyer,* April 1994); "Why Cross-Selling Hasn't Worked" (in *The American Lawyer,* October 1993); "Measuring Your Marketing Success" (in *Professional Marketing,* September 1993); "Satisfaction Guaranteed" (as "The New Value Billing," in *The American Lawyer,* May 1994).